TIE ME TO
THE MAST

TIE ME TO THE MAST

... the football season
has begun

David Johnson

SPORTS
BOOKS

Published by SportsBooks Ltd

Copyright: David Johnson © 2008
First published September 2008

SportsBooks Limited
PO Box 422
Cheltenham
GL50 2YN
United Kingdom
Tel: 01242 256755
Fax: 01242 254694
e-mail randall@sportsbooks.ltd.uk
Website www.sportsbooks.ltd.uk

Stanza from Philip Larkin's poem *This be the Verse*
on page 120
by kind permission Faber & Faber

A CIP catalogue record for this book is available from
the British Library.

ISBN 9781899807 73 4

Printed by Creative Print and Design, Wales

For Alison and Harry with all my love.

CHAPTER 1

If you ever want to cheer yourself up, don't come to Morrisons in Stoke-on-Trent.

I'm sitting in the car park watching the rain and the people and the scrotty, grey birds hopping in and out of the exhaust-coated bushes. I've just seen a *rat* sloping past, for God's sake.

In a minute I'll go through the ever-so-slightly mistimed automatic doors and into the shop to buy lunch. Past the café ('your cholesterol levels doubled – or your money back'), past the stands where wide boys sell double glazing or one hundred and twenty-seven channels of crap to people who can't really afford double glazing or one hundred and twenty-seven channels of crap, past the checkout belts relentlessly feeding multi-packs of crisps, doughnuts and improbably-coloured fizzy drinks to fat customers, and on to the sandwich kiosk.

It's pretty much the same as most lunchtimes. Except this one's a bit different. It's the end of June, and I'm feeling a familiar twitch of excitement. It's just a niggle; a little internal tweak at the moment, but it's there. Just over a month upwind, I can smell the new football season.

I wonder if any of the other beaten-looking customers can sense it, but I know at least some of them can – it's what makes us fans and brings us together. Maybe the dad and the son from the family screaming at each other by the tinned fruit, those youths in the three-quarter lengths, and some of the unfeasibly large number of people in wheelchairs or with sticks, disfigurements or care in the community ticks. Football fans from across the city are coming out of hibernation.

I leave the shop, only just remembering to sidestep the malicious doors, and hunch my shoulders against the rain as I scuttle back to the car and skim through *The Sentinel*.

Bizarrely, these days I can't seem to turn a page without licking my finger first. I don't recall having a similar problem before I turned forty, or having to throw down books unread in frustration at not being able to turn past page three. I remember my grandad doing the same thing, which must have annoyed the librarians who had to take back his westerns with every page corner smudged and corroded by copious amounts of pensioner spittle. Perhaps it's an age thing, and on your fortieth birthday all your digits dry out as if some internal tap has been turned off.

Anyway, I learn from the paper that, in a fit of destructive criticism, arsonists have destroyed a community art project, more health service jobs are going, the city council has been accepting hangovers as a valid reason for throwing a sickie and a bloke has been done for headbutting an opponent during a six-a-side football game.

I scan the letters from people complaining about an impressive range of topics including, strangely, the number of people who write to the paper complaining.

The back pages are full of doom and gloom about the prospects for Stoke City's forthcoming season. So far our only new signing has been Jon Parkin from Hull, an overweight striker who has fallen out of favour at a number of clubs, reportedly because of his penchant for lard and beer. Personally, I don't care if the lad isn't shy of a pie and comes onto the pitch with ketchup and egg stains on his shirt as long as he bangs the goals in; but one portly player does not a summer make.

Even though last season we only just missed out on a play-off place for the promised land of the Premier League, the fans are getting restless at the lack of transfer activity.

Reading between the lines, you can sense manager Tony

Pulis's increasing desperation at missing out on a string of close-season targets. In fact he's probably trying to find the number of the headbutting six-a-sider right now in his attempts to bring in a combative midfielder.

It's the Monday before the start of the season and I can see a dark cloud looming.

I need my wife to give me a pass-out for the first game away at Cardiff. Usually, this would be a matter for delicate negotiation and I would end up agreeing to take over all childcare duties for a couple of days. But there's a complication. She has already agreed I can have a night out with Ash on Friday, which will be one of only a handful of boozy nights I've managed in the twenty months since our son was born. I just can't see her going for it. It's going to have to be some blag to get this one signed off.

'I'm going to write a book about being a Stoke fan.'

'Excuse me?'

'Uhhh ... I'm writing a book.'

'Okay. Right.'

'The point is, I need to go to the first game or no-one'll take me seriously.'

'But it's the day after you're leaving me on my own, to go out with Ash.'

'I've got to do that as well.'

'Why?'

'Because we'll be talking about football and Ash'll come up with a load of really good stuff for the book.'

Eventually, she buckles.

But if I'm going to avoid the divorce courts, I'm going to have to face the inevitable fallout of my deception – I really *am* going to have to write a book about being a football fan.

CHAPTER 2

People often say that football is just a game, and that great tragedies and global news events put the sport into perspective. These people are, of course, idiots, and should be ignored – if not roundly abused.

For football fans, there are three vital strands to life: work, private life and team. For us to be able to interact effectively with society as a whole, at least one of these needs to be working well.

If your team is made up of cretinous workhorses who have lost the last eighteen games and your wife is having an affair, you could just about get by if you are the rising star at the office, winning promotion after promotion and taking home six figures.

If your wife then tells you she wants a divorce so she can marry her lover and you get sacked, but your team might, against all the odds, make the play-offs, you could probably still function as a human being. When, however, your now ex-wife announces she is pregnant, you lose out to someone called Bailie on the job serving in McDonald's and your team are relegated on goal difference on the last day of the season, it's time to choke yourself to death on your half-time pie screaming: 'This is all because of you, you useless bastards!'

On reflection, I realise it may be difficult to scream anything intelligible and choke yourself to death at the same time, but you know what I mean.

I'm just saying that football matters. When Andy's fiancée upped and left him, did he wallow in self-pity and drink himself senseless night after night? Well, yes, actually, but the *first* thing he did was drive down to Stoke from Manchester, park up at the Britannia Stadium and spend a quiet hour sitting by the statue of Sir Stanley Matthews.

A few weeks ago a friend of mine killed himself by walking in front of a truck on the M6. He was Celtic through and through and just about the most intelligent, gentlest guy I've ever known. In spite of the priest's assurances during the funeral that Ade had now shut his eyes and was sleeping peacefully with our Lord Jesus Christ, I couldn't stop imagining the moment of impact and wondering how Ade looked to the driver in the split second before. As the lorries rumbled by outside the church, I forced my mind to switch channel and started thinking about the season ahead.

People find comfort in a lot of things, and some convince themselves of the existence of an afterlife, but that day it was football that helped me. Like I say – it matters.

It's here. As I set off for Cardiff, my mouth's hangover dry from my night out, it's hot as hell in the car and I start to sweat strong imported lager and whisky. Last night I'd suggested to Ash we go into town to look at young girls in short skirts, but he pointed out we now have the internet for that sort of thing, so what was the point? I accepted the logic of his argument and we walked to the local.

I feel a swell of panic as I realise I'm driving over the spot where Ade died. But it's gone almost as soon as I notice it and I start to enjoy the journey and the sun. Radio 5 Live is putting out wall-to-wall football and instantly I'm once again part of that global community. So what if we've sold some of our key players, we've got a team full of loan signings, kids and journeymen sliding down the back end of their careers? The fans may be starting to revolt, but I know each car I see with a Stoke scarf in it is inhabited by people feeling the same irrational, unlooked-for, wonderful anticipation as me.

Stoke and Cardiff both have a poor reputation for football

violence (or a good one, I suppose, depending which way you look at it). Academics point to the link between multiple deprivation and casual violence, although less charitable amateur scholars conclude the two clubs are just followed by a higher-than-average proportion of violent, drug-crazed psychopaths.

Whatever, the two cities have both been crippled economically in the last century. In 1970, fifty thousand people worked in the North Staffordshire pottery industry. Now it's more like ten thousand. Tens of thousands more worked in the area's coalfields or were employed at the steelworks. Now precisely no people work in these industries.

From the 1990s, Stoke-on-Trent could only look on enviously as regeneration money poured into the Welsh capital and the population's skills, health and wealth improved. The cash is now starting to roll into Stoke (the Government and European Union must have run out of other places to throw money at), but we're still years behind Cardiff.

About sixteen per cent of working-age people in Stoke-on-Trent aren't in employment, education or training, the highest proportion out of every comparable city in the country. About fifteen per cent are on incapacity benefit, compared to nine per cent in Cardiff. Teenage pregnancy rates are higher in Stoke-on-Trent than in Cardiff, as are violent crime, robbery and arson rates.

The notable exceptions are car theft and theft from cars, which are much more common in Cardiff. Perversely, I feel slightly ashamed at the poor performance of our car thieves and almost wish they would take a bit more pride in their work so we could all wallow in our own crapness more completely.

All this doom and gloom may give the impression that my city is full of pregnant teenagers speeding around in wheelchairs robbing people at knifepoint (and admittedly a stroll round Morrisons at lunchtime may reinforce this impression), but things are changing. I can sometimes go weeks without being beaten up, and it may be a dump in parts, but it's my dump and I love it.

There's still half an hour to go before kick-off, but inside the ground there's that very specific tone of expectant buzz you only get on the first day of the season. The atmosphere's building and I feel at home in a stadium I've never been to before.

I do my usual opening game new tattoo survey and I'm pleased to see a good number of freshly-inked Stoke crests on proud display, some still crusting over, they are so recent. The comforting old favourites are still there, too, like the mountain of a bloke with 'Made In Stoke' written on his neck.

Although I've seen him countless times at the ground, I can't remember whether the tattoo actually says 'Made In Stoke-on-Trent' and the '-on-Trent' bit is hidden beneath his collar, but I decide against asking him. The strangest new entry to the tat gallery is a woman who looks like a librarian or careers officer with an obviously new, beautifully depicted koala bear on her calf. I like to think it's the result of a rare drunken night on a summer holiday to Australia.

A few yards away, where our end butts up against a home stand to form a corner of the ground, there's a band of Cardiff nutters giving wanker signs and drawing their fingers across their throats when they catch the eye of any Stoke fans. They're dressed in the Burberry, Stone Island and Henri Lloyd gear beloved of hooligans and wannabes across the country, except for one guy in his thirties wearing crisp shorts and a square shirt who's here with his boy, who must be six or seven.

The guy looks like a driving instructor or teacher, and I feel sorry for him mistakenly buying a ticket in the naughty pen. Then he sees me looking at him and he's out of his seat, nearly knocking his son over in the process, screaming abuse and pointing his finger at me, his spittle catching the sun quite attractively. I smile pleasantly at him, which for some reason doesn't seem to calm him down. From that point, the driving instructor spits his demented rage at any Stoke fans he can see, causing much hilarity. God knows what his son will grow up like.

But I love it – it's sunny, there's an edge to the atmosphere, the players are out and the whistle is at the ref's lips. Tie me to the mast; another season's about to start.

As soon as the game kicks off, it's obvious they have better players than us. But we survive the initial onslaught and in the twenty-seventh minute Ryan Shawcross, a nineteen-year-old we signed on a six-month loan from Manchester United less than twenty-four hours ago, sweeps the ball into the net from a corner. Eight hundred Stokies burst with that first great communal eruption of joy of the season.

Of course I miss the goal because I'm too busy watching the driving instructor, who by this point has worked himself up into such a lather of hatred it's a wonder he doesn't actually explode, covering surprised supporters in a twenty-seat radius with barely-identifiable body parts.

So that's a three hundred and thirty mile round trip to miss the first goal of the season, but I don't care. As we launch into a thunderous version of *Delilah* and my eardrums press into my head from the glorious sound, I just know this is going to be our day. As the game wears on, keeper Steve Simonsen makes some outstanding saves, but Cardiff's threat fades.

Throughout the second half, we entertain ourselves by singing songs of a nature unlikely to improve the already-strained Anglo-Welsh relations in the ground. Then, with a couple of minutes to go, the ref gives Cardiff a dodgy penalty and the plummeting of eight hundred hearts is almost audible. Yet again, our day is going to be ruined at the last, and the Cardiff crazies a few yards away will joyously rub our noses in it.

But the penalty is weak, Simmo makes a good first save and pulls off nothing short of a miracle to keep out the rebound and all of a sudden we've won the game. Adrenalin-saturated relief surges through every singing Stoke fan as we mercilessly humiliate the home fans.

On the drive back I get one of those rare moments of calm contentment. We won against the odds, the evening sun is washing everything with colour and later I'll share a bottle of wine with my wife and pop my head round Harry's door to watch my beautiful little boy sleeping. Perfect.

At half-time during the game there was a strange little episode that has stayed with me.

The announcer read through a list of Cardiff fans who had died during the close season. One was a lifelong supporter who had killed himself after renewing his season ticket, which seemed particularly bad timing from a financial point of view, although I suppose you can't take it with you. We were given a catalogue of misfortunes and family tragedies that had stalked the poor bloke in the months running up to his suicide, and the list was so long it made even the most maudlin soap opera storyline seem unambitious. But something about the matter-of-fact summary of a life meant there was never even a hint of the usual gallows humour of the football crowd.

Another was a young guy in the forces who had died in a helicopter crash just days before, but all his mates were in the stands watching the game because they felt it was the right thing to do.

I don't know what motivates the club to collate this grim register – or relatives and friends to contribute to it – but instead of being mawkish it was subtly moving and uniting, and it threw the importance of the link between club and fan into sharp relief.

So tell me what you like about football – that it's just a game played by overpaid, thick-as-mince prima donnas and watched by underpaid, thick-as-mince Neanderthals. But don't tell me it doesn't matter.

CHAPTER 3

You really wouldn't think loading a dishwasher could be such a contentious issue.

Or maybe you would, I don't know. Maybe I really *am* so bad at it I deserve to be horsewhipped in the town square while efficient loaders throw ten-in-one powerball supershine tablets at my sorry arse.

Anyway, the morning of the first home game of the season starts badly. Alison is once again displeased at my kitchen utensil washing policy. In recent months I have learned that only an idiot would fill dishes from the outside in and that there are elders in as yet undiscovered tribes in the Amazon rainforest, with no electricity and indeed no crockery, who would feed anyone who placed a fork prong-end down in the cutlery basket to the piranhas. So this morning we've moved on.

'I don't think you should put that pestle and mortar in there,' she says.

'Why not?'

'It might chip.'

'But it's solid granite.'

'I just don't think you should.'

'Al, it's made out of one of the hardest materials known to man, forged at thousands of degrees centigrade beneath the Earth's crust. Why do you think they make pestles and mortars – which are specifically designed to crush and grind softer materials – out of granite and not, say, glass? If you think granite is going to chip, are you going to take all the glasses out?'

'I just worry that it's very porous.'

'Listen, Al, I did A-level geology, and okay, I only got a

D, but believe me, a less porous material you are unlikely to find.'

'Stop being an argumentative arse and take it out.'

I stop being an argumentative arse, take it out and make a mental note to find out which bit is the pestle and which bit is the mortar.

So the omens aren't good. The opening home game of the season is always sunny. Except today; it's still August, but it's grey and windy and freezing, with bad-tempered showers slapping you in the face every few minutes.

Maybe I have rose-tinted memories about past curtain-raisers, like most of us have about crisp, snowy childhood winters, those endless, drowsy, sun-baked school summer holidays and Louise Fisher's thick, grey, woolly tights. Okay, that last one may just be me, but you get my drift.

We moved to the Britannia Stadium ten years ago, when the trend to sell off city and town centre grounds for housing and build new ones as part of out-of-town retail and industrial parks was a couple of years old.

You'd think a decade would be a reasonable length of time to figure out what to do with a piece of land, but the site of the old Victoria Ground is still scrub, although plans for housing have just been submitted. When my dad first took me to see Stoke about thirty-five years ago, the Vic seemed like a huge, mystical magnet, drawing in streams of people from the town centre and down the terraced streets, everyone walking at the pace of the person in front as if being steadily sucked into the stadium in a trance. Now it's gone and the overgrown plot looks small and unimportant and feels like a marquee the day after a wedding.

The Britannia Stadium is on a perma-blustery hill, hemmed in by the A50 and A500 on two sides and a commercial estate and car parking on the other two. To get to it on foot from the town, you walk along a road which in a stretch of a few hundred yards bridges no fewer than ten carriageways of main road and exit and entry slips, which gives you some idea of how fan-friendly its location is. In fact a few days ago, a 16-year-old supporter was hit by a car and killed as he tried to take a short cut across one of the slip roads. The police are out before this evening's game handing out flyers warning people of the dangers of car-dodging, and Stoke flags and scarves tied to a road sign in tribute to the dead boy flap and slap against the cold metal.

I park near the old ground and walk up the track by the River Trent. Squint your eyes in one direction and you could be strolling by an idyllic Cotswold stream, but open them again and you can see the factories behind the willows and the shopping trolleys and traffic cones jutting iceberg-like out of the water. The grumble of the A500 a few yards away doesn't exactly help the image either. On the twenty-foot concrete embankment which carries the main road above and to the left, someone has daubed 'IS THIS WHAT YOU CALL CHANGE?', which somehow seems appropriate in a grim-up-north sort of way.

Soon I'm passing the Sainsbury's warehouse and other exotic North Staffordshire attractions like the incinerator, following the canal, crossing the railway bridge, leaning into Cardiac Hill and then there's the inevitable smack in the face by the wind as I reach stadium level.

The lazy, journalistic cliché is to brand grounds of the Brit's generation as 'soulless', but I'm not sure that's true. Yes, the atmosphere is dire – especially compared to the Victoria Ground, which generated intimidating passion and volume even when it was only half full. Yes, the corners need filling in, and yes it's so windy up there they've had to rename Chicago the Quite Blustery City.

But it has a certain bleak spirit and inaccessibility in which we take a perverse sort of pride. Not soulless, just not brilliantly thought out because of a desperate need to move out of a crumbling ground ten years ago before the Government grants dried up.

As well as adhering to the new all-seating laws, the club's official line at the time was that they wanted to create a ground where families felt comfortable, although how much genuine effort went into this is open to argument.

Personally, I'm not keen on making stadia family-orientated. I like an atmosphere with an edge, like at the Cardiff game last week, and I enjoy the freedom to scream the odd obscenity with little chance of being locked up or frowned at. For a fortnight we keep a lid on our frustration, anger and insecurity and then every other Saturday it all gets released in an orgasmic geyser of fucks and wanks as Mama Sidibe spoons another chance into the crowd.

And this is surely healthy. Life could be decidedly unpleasant if we all said what we felt on the other days of the week.

'I'm sure you've got time to finish that report by Friday, Dave.'

'As a matter of fact I haven't. I already spend far too much of my rapidly-shortening life at this desk. You can stick your poxy job up your arse.'

Or: 'Would you like to go large with that meal?'

'No I wouldn't, you moron. The only reason I have ordered this pile of regurgitated animal clippings is because your employers spend billions of pounds on advertising to dupe me into coming here and because the pictures over your head don't even bear a passing resemblance to the crap you actually churn out. If you'd paid attention in school, you dead-beat, you wouldn't have to stand there all day serving poisonous filth to people like me who are too stupid to stay away.'

As I say, the omens aren't good, and to cap it all we're playing Charlton, who came down from the Premier League last season and who are favourites to go straight back up, and the game is being broadcast live – an opportunity to be humiliated in front of the nation which Stoke usually grab with both hands.

We annihilate them for the first fifteen minutes before running out of steam, and then early in the second half they score from a lucky free kick that deflects wildly off the arse of their defender Jonathan Fortune, who played for us on loan last season. I scrunch down in my seat and prepare for the inevitable.

But miraculously, just two minutes later, Ricardo Fuller, our one genuinely talented player, loses his man, drifts across the edge of the penalty area and curls a beauty into the far corner. Then Parkin comes on (I swear he's brushing pie crumbs from his shirt as he gets off the bench) and five minutes later, his gut a split-second out of time with the rest of his movements, he turns his man beautifully and slides the ball past the keeper.

Charlton besiege our goal and once again Simmo pulls off a string of fine saves, but the whistle goes and, bugger me, we're top of the league. That night I sleep well, comfortable in the knowledge we didn't embarrass ourselves on telly and that the mortar is the bit that gets bashed and the pestle is the bit that does the bashing.

CHAPTER 4

It doesn't last, of course. A few weeks later, grey reality has reasserted itself.

The day before the Southampton away game, our inept striker Vincent Pericard is sent to prison for four months. But the fans' wild celebrations at a stroke of luck that will keep the buffoon out of the team for at least eight weeks are short-lived as we lose the game 3-2.

Pericard, for the record, in a move unlikely to dent the stereotype of footballers being just a little bit thick, told police his step-dad had been driving the car caught doing one hundred and three miles per hour on the A38. Poor old Vincent hadn't banked on the inspired genius of the British copper, however, and some bright spark – surely a direct descendant of Sherlock himself – decided to check. A quick call to France later, in which Monsieur Pericard happily confirmed he hadn't been to the U.K. for three years, and V.P.'s fate was sealed.

Shortly after the Southampton game we sell our captain, Danny Higginbotham, to Sunderland for £3m. Pulis keeps whingeing about how hard it is to sign decent players, but he seems to find it easy enough to sell ours.

Shortly after a dull 0-0 draw with Wolves, my wife's one-woman campaign to improve kitchen etiquette takes an un-nerving detour from dishwashers to resealable tabs. Apparently I have been failing to use the sticky labels thoughtfully provided by tea bag manufacturers, leading to a criminal loss of freshness during storage.

Patiently, I explain she is a gullible but innocent victim

caught in the crossfire of a marketing war between rival companies and that she really shouldn't lose any sleep over it. The only people to benefit from sealing in freshness, I say, are senior managers at tea bag makers and the shareholders of the companies they work for. I add that it's impossible to use the stupid things anyway, because within a day their self-adhesive qualities are precisely nil as a result of all the tea dust that sticks to them.

I don't get quite the reaction I hoped for after this master-ful display of killer logic, and in a worrying escalation of hos-tilities she berates me for not using the same strips of tape on packets of pasta. I think about giving her my considered opin-ion that these are, if possible, even less useful than the gim-micks foisted on us by tea manufacturers because it is impos-sible to open a packet of penne without it splitting completely, rendering a two-inch piece of Sellotape about as effective as a sticking plaster on one of those farmers who insist on losing limbs in medieval-looking machinery and who then hop four miles over fields to the hospital, carrying their severed legs under their arms. She's starting to get that strange twitch in her eye again, though, so I decide to drop the subject.

Anyway, I digress. Before the game away at Hull, Pulis says it's difficult to get players to come to Stoke-on-Trent. Reasonably, many people see this as a dark hint that the city itself, rather than the club, is unattractive to anyone under the age of seventy-five who can afford to live anywhere else. A dump, in other words, in spite of an ever-increasing number of lap-dancing bars – the preferred entertainment for today's discerning professional footballer.

The theory doesn't really stack up, though. For example Hull City, based in the only urban area to feature more often in the top twenty worst places to live in the Western Hemisphere list than Stoke-on-Trent, have just managed to sign Jay-Jay Okocha, the former Bolton and Nigeria legend.

Venice Stoke ain't, but it should certainly be able to give Hull, Bolton and Lagos a run for their money.

The game ends 1-1, and that's followed by a 0-0 draw of such crushing, energy-sapping, debilitating dullness against Barnsley that it will, perversely, live in my memory forever. If we're stupid enough to pay to watch this, I'm convinced people would queue overnight in the rain to snaffle up tickets for the Dulux UK Paint-Drying Championships.

Within ten minutes, Robbo is watching the Champions League on his mobile, and Andy is playing Snake on his. Had this game been staged before the advent of cellular telecommunications, police, baffled at the lack of crowd control required after the match, would have found thirteen thousand corpses slumped in the stands, some with slit wrists, some strangled by belts and shoelaces and some asphyxiated by the sheer weight of boredom.

When I get home I channel my frustration in the most constructive way I know in an attempt to save myself from crap football-induced insanity.

> To: Consumer Services, Tetley Tea.
> Dear consumer services adviser,
> Please advise this consumer as to the benefits of those self-adhesive strips you kindly provide with your packets of tea bags. If memory serves, your adverts talk about sealing in freshness. How fresh does it have to be? It's a dried product, for fuck's sake.
> I'm told by people who should know about these things that the most highly-prized tea is known as pu-erh, made with aged, semi-oxidised leaves grown in China's Yunnan Province. The rarest examples are one hundred years old and for a 350g pack from the 1950s – wrapped in leaves, mind you, not plastic with an annoying adhesive strip which, rather than sealing

in freshness as you claim, just collects dust and falls off after two days – you would have to pay £8,000.

It seems the Chinese, who, let's be honest, should know a thing or two about tea, aren't as concerned about capturing that just-picked flavour as your marketing department.

In the interest of scientific advancement, I performed a taste test on my wife (I appreciate this sounds slightly pornographic, but bear with me). I made two cups of tea using the classic bag-in-a-mug technique (same size mug, add boiling water, ten revolutions with the spoon, spoon out to allow the bag to rotate freely and to reduce heat loss, wait thirty seconds, two medium squeezes against the side of the mug and out – I don't have to tell you guys this, *you're* the experts). One of the bags I used was bursting with sealed-in freshness after being stored in textbook Tetley fashion, while the other one was rescued from my drawer at work. It had been there, on a nest of rubber bands and fluff, with no plastic packaging and no annoying adhesive tab, for at least seven weeks.

It was no surprise to me that my wife could tell no difference but, when pressed, plumped for the delicate flavours of flat-pack office furniture and stationery. And this is a woman with the heightened senses of a Ninja who can smell alcohol on my breath at twenty metres on a breezy day.

I would be grateful if you could send me the results of the rigorous scientific studies you undoubtedly carried out before foisting resealable tabs on the tea-drinkers of Great Britain. Research into profit margins doesn't count.

Kind regards,

David Johnson

Feeling slightly better, I can't help thinking that, one way or another, this is going to be a seminal season. We're being roundly reviled by other fans, clubs and pundits for playing awful, negative football, we're being roundly reviled by our *own* fans for playing awful, negative football, our manager can't buy any players, there are rumours of rifts between various directors and Tony Pulis, crowds are down, the atmosphere in the stadium is terrible and fans are split into pro- and anti-Pulis camps.

But in spite of everything, after a tough start to the season, with games against some of the teams tipped for promotion, we're still in the play-off positions. If Pulis can defy his critics when the transfer window opens in January and actually persuade two or three more-than-usually-stupid players to come here then who knows what could happen? I don't know if we're going to get promoted or relegated or if there's going to be blood on the boardroom floor, but something big is going to happen; you can just smell it.

CHAPTER 5

Ian is a great believer in the power of positive thinking. Or, put another way, he's a bit simple. Anyone who still believes that things will generally turn out for the best after watching Stoke for as long as my brother-in-law must have a medically worrying ability for self-delusion. For Ian, the glass is not just half full, it is overflowing with liquid optimism pouring into his lap to leave a wet patch of excitement.

But now even *his* faith is draining away, the early season energy is evaporating into the grey sky above the Brit, and the fans look like the losing team of rabbits in the Duracell advert.

It's interesting how often discussions about football use the language of faith. Comparing the sport to religion – worshipping at our cathedrals every week, communal songs of praise, fanaticism, the Hand of God and so on – has long since passed into cliché.

I'm not even sure how valid the comparisons really are, and football is arguably a more worthwhile investment of faith than religion. I'm pretty sure I could prove the existence of football, for example, although granted I would have struggled at the Barnsley game, and I would guess marginally fewer people have been killed in conflicts sparked by sporting loyalty than religious allegiance.

I'm always slightly in awe of how people who are deeply religious can be so sure they've picked the right team, as it were; the maths is just so stacked against them. There are more than one hundred religions in Borneo alone, for God's (or Allah's or Buddha's or whoever else's) sake. How can the 2.1 billion Christians, for example, be so sure they know better than the world's 1.3 billion Muslims, 900 million Hindus, 376 million Buddhists, 23 million Sikhs and 14 million Jews? That's not to mention the millions of others who follow the Baha'i faith, Confucianism, Jainism, Zoroastrianism, Shinto, Taoism, or Dale Wintonism.

But this is where the similarities with football begin. Fans put blind faith in their team in the face of overwhelming evidence and experience that they will be let down time and again and that their prayers will almost invariably go unanswered. As in religion, where we bestow our unshakeable allegiance is largely determined by where we live and who our family support, and intermarriage between rival faiths draws comment. And, just as is happening with religion, modern technology is having an impact.

In football you have the gloryhunters, who support teams hundreds of miles from their homes because they've seen them winning week in, week out on Sky, and then you have the power and the glory hunters, who, thanks to satellite television and the internet, can pick and choose between any number of faiths to help them come to terms with their own mortality.

Personally, I don't need the promise of an afterlife to get through the day. That's not to say I'm overly thrilled about the prospect of turning tits-up, mind you. After the age of thirty, time speeds up alarmingly and approaches terminal velocity at forty when it rips through the gears in an unstoppable race towards the coffin.

The frustrating inevitability of your own death, though, isn't really a problem for me. I have accepted the fact that I will never be a rock god, film star, astronaut or train driver. I have even accepted that, unless she's had a real run of bad luck, I will never take Louise Fisher's virginity. Perhaps the hardiest of youth's impossible dreams was the certainty that I would see Stoke play at the highest level. Some time over the last five or ten years, though, that too has gone.

At best, I now only have about forty years left to see Stoke in the Champions League or the Premier League, or in fact do anything vaguely interesting. The prospects are even grimmer when you take off a few years for drooling senility and the inability to go to games because of incontinence. When I first started going to matches, the players seemed impossibly old; now most of them are just boys, and even the refs look like school prefects.

Master criminal Vincent Pericard is due to be released next week, and just before the Plymouth game Pulis appeals for tolerance from the fans towards the Moriarty of the footballing fraternity. I can't quite decide what he means by this. Is he afraid fans will storm the bastions of justice, outraged that Pericard has been released early and in with a shout of playing for us again? Or is he afraid we hold a grudge against the player because he has spent the last few weeks doing his best to miss kitchen duty, rather than playing for us doing his best to miss open goals? Pulis doesn't seem to realise fans will worship mass murderers if they play well; what they generally can't tolerate, though, is strikers who don't score.

The game itself is a strange affair. We're winning 1-0 at half-time before giving away two comedy goals early in the second half. A sizeable section of the crowd turns, and it's not just isolated or uncoordinated protest this time. You can always identify the moment run-of-the-mill dissatisfaction turns to something more serious. The boos start here and there, but instead of petering out as they have done at previous matches, they smoulder and catch and spread and merge. Within a few seconds the sound is sinister and stoppable only by a goal.

It comes in the sixty-sixth minute, and it's followed by another to give us a 3-2 win. Coming from behind to win is as good as it gets for a football fan, but for some reason this is different. Usually, the relief and joy makes for a short walk to the car. Everyone's laughing, talking quickly, telling each other about a game we've all seen. But this evening it's all low-key mumbles and grumbles, and it seems to take a week to get to where we've parked. We're higher in the league than we could have expected, but there's something about the way we've been playing that is just so boring, ugly and unconvincing, that anyone over the age of six is struggling to raise any enthusiasm.

On the radio after the game, Pulis apologises with heavy sarcasm to moaning fans for being 'only' fifth in the league with a threadbare squad full of kids and loan players.

'IT'S YOUR FAULT WE HAVEN'T GOT A SQUAD, YOU MORON – YOU'RE THE MANAGER!' I scream at the car radio.

How *dare* he take the piss out of the fans? I mean *really* how dare he? He must be on thin ice with his chairman, he's living on borrowed time with the fans and it seems to me he's going to need all the allies he can get in the storms ahead. He just comes across as being too easily pleased and he's either unconcerned about the way we're playing or his concept of entertainment is completely out of kilter with anyone not institutionalised on a permanent basis. Maybe that's it. Maybe what he wants to watch is just completely different to what *I* want to watch. Maybe he goes home and laughs at his *Krankies*, *Last of the Summer Wine* and *My Family* DVDs so hard he soils himself.

He reminds me of an oatcake shop I go to in Stoke sometimes. The owners have taken great pride in framing a health and safety certificate which says their premises achieved a satisfactory level of hygiene following the last inspection in 1920 or whenever. Now, I'm no expert, but I'm ready to bet 'satisfactory' wasn't the highest possible plaudit available from the boys and girls with the white coats and swabs. There are times when satisfactory just doesn't quite cut the mustard. Having an oatcake prepared by a decidedly grubby bloke sweating into the batter is one of them, and scraping points off rubbish teams in a manner that brings shame on your club and your city is another.

My mood isn't really helped by draws at Leicester and West Brom – we *always* beat West Brom, no matter how much better than us they are (and they usually are). We're now seventh in the table.

But things brighten up with a deserved and entertaining 2-1 win against an in-form Colchester, and they become positively radiant when Vincent Pericard is sent back to jail the following week after his electronic tag 'accidentally' comes off for a second time. Genius.

CHAPTER 6

We want another baby and, if I don't want to be changing nappies when I'm a toothless, wrinkled old man, I need to get cracking sharpish. But the prospect of having another child raises deep moral issues of such complexity that my libido retreats into a dark corner of my brain and I find it difficult to maintain the required level of arousal to achieve a successful impregnation.

The love I have for my son fills me entirely, so how could I possibly have another baby? There's simply no emotional spare capacity there. Anyone who says he supports two teams is not a genuine supporter at all. And what if one child started doing much better at school than the other one? Would I be tempted to switch allegiance like some glory hunting tosspot?

I should talk to Alison about it, I know, especially as she was a season ticket holder for as long as I was before Harry was born. Even now our ticket is meant to be shared so she can go to the game if she wants, but, carelessly, this agreement slips my mind on a weekly basis. She knows what it's like to be a genuine fan, so surely she'd understand? But having a partner who is knowledgeable and passionate about football also adds to the list of potential subjects for argument – a list which already includes politics, religion, whether her own definition of excessive drinking should be applied to anyone else, the exact baked-on grime conditions under which you should switch from 'economy' to 'normal' programme on a Hotpoint dishwasher, why it really *is* vital to Hoover the entire house when we're late for the plane which will take us on our only holiday of the year, and whether it really *is* inappropriate to ogle anyone's breasts other than your wife's.

Incidentally, no-one's asked Harry what he thinks about this new baby scheme, and if they did I think he'd be livid. For months, he's been screaming: 'MINE!' whenever anyone even looks at one of his toys, books, parents or anything else and launching at the offending baby, toddler, parent, grandparent or domestic pet with both fists.

'MY FIRE ENGINE! MY STORY! MY DADDY!'

Alison says his psychopathic streak must come from my side of the family, but at least he's got out of the biting stage. It was getting embarrassing having to call the RSPCA every week to give him enough sedative to allow the officer to prise his jaws open and remove his teeth from Nana's arm or the lower leg of the perfectly-behaved little girl with the curly hair at nursery. It was like being father to Hannibal Lecter, and I'm not convinced any addition to the family would be welcomed with open arms by my son, especially considering he would be old enough, by the time of the new arrival, to have mastered quite advanced knife skills or even, if impregnation takes a few months and if his current level of interest in extreme violence is maintained, competence with firearms.

It's a bloody minefield, so I decide to ask the lads at the match for their opinions. The consensus seems to be that I'm a prick.

Oh, if you're interested, we lose 4-2 at home to Sheffield Wednesday.

CHAPTER 7

By mid October, we're being ridiculed in the press for our negative tactics and penchant for wellying the ball as far out of defence as possible towards our strikers, preferably missing out the midfield altogether.

Some fans are disenchanted watching games where the ball can touch the ground four times in ninety minutes, but I believe this is a stroke of fiscal genius from Pulis. We are just a couple of training sessions away from being able to do away with four or even five players altogether – potentially a massive saving for the club. If the killjoys at the Football Association insist fielding only six or seven players is against the rules, we could stick a few McDonald's rejects in the middle on the minimum wage and spend the rest on pies made with the finest and rarest ingredients for Parkin.

Not content with sneering at our football club, media types have now got the entire city in their sights.

Stoke-on-Trent is rated as the thirteenth-worst place to live in the UK on Channel 4's *Location, Location, Location* – that godawful show for people obsessed with house prices which every week follows some achingly trendy and successful young professional couple who have a £750,000 budget to find a cottage with enough land for Phoebe's pony and a 'crash pad' near the airport. I swear to God, if anyone used the phrase crash pad in a conversation with me I would laugh in his or her achingly successful face.

Anyway, in this special edition of the programme the big-boned girl who, in my considered opinion, is slightly porcine, wears too much make-up, has some strange 1961 hair-do and looks as if she could turn into the insane psychopath from

Misery, and her oily-faced buffoon of a male sidekick tell us their crack team of researchers has compiled the definitive list of crap places to live.

'Around 3.5m tourists come to Stoke each year to see the internationally renowned pottery industry,' they tell us down their noses.

'They can't all be lost. What amazes me is that eighty per cent of them come back again!' Oh, how we laughed.

'Stoke is one of the most depressed – and depressing – areas in the country.'

They trot out the usual reasons why Stoke-on-Trent always appears in these lists and then tell us that one in five families in the city is homeless. Now I'm no statistician or human geography professor, and I'm used to figures that tend to suggest people should consider moving to Mordor before asking estate agents for North Staffordshire brochures, but *one in five?*

Surely I would have noticed this. Surely every time I walked into the city centre for a sandwich and a jumbo sausage roll I would dislodge a bow wave of beggars and crack addicts with every step. And when I finally arrived at Three Cooks I would have to launch myself at the door handle and drag myself in using my last ounce of strength to kick off a motley selection of wizened crones and salivating children who look like extras from a zombie film. It's plainly ridiculous, but none of the self-satisfied Oxbridge graduates working on the show seems to have batted an eyelid.

Over the years, people have fallen over themselves in their eagerness to have a dig at Stoke-on-Trent.

In *English Journey*, published in 1934, JB Priestley called the city grim, smoky, dingy, dirty, shabby, preposterous and, in sum, 'extremely ugly'.

And in 1961's *Potbank – A social enquiry into life in the Potteries*, novelist and journalist Mervyn Jones's impression of the city is one of 'sad, drab uniformity ... adjustment to steady greyness is a Potteries gift.' You can say that again; how else could so many of the residents sit through the dull tripe we too often have to watch every other Saturday, year in, year out?

'To be frank,' he goes on, 'there is still a good deal of smoke about. Looking down on the city from a height – say, from the surrounded old village of Penkhull – you must pick out the landmarks through a drifting blur, even on a Sunday. A science student told me he had analysed a sample of air and recorded a horrifying, unrivalled percentage of carbon.

'I heard it rumoured that a smokeless zone is to be decreed in Stoke-on-Trent. I should say that this would be the most unrealistic enterprise since American prohibition.'

You get the impression Mervyn wasn't exactly in the market for romance during his stay, either.

On a visit to a pub he noticed the early customers were all women.

He says: 'They had the type of face I kept seeing in the Potteries – a face which appeared to have been put in a vice and squeezed from above and below, making the flesh ooze out in soft pink bulges of cheeks and chins.' Mmm, attractive. Jones's assessment is, of course, complete rubbish and possibly actionable in a court of law. I'm *married* to a Potteries girl and I can categorically state she only looks as if her face has been squeezed in a vice from below.

In his 1970s series *The Buildings Of England*, art historian Nikolaus Pevsner wrote that what had happened to the city's built environment was an 'urban tragedy'.

He describes the Potteries as 'the seat of great industry and the fourteenth largest city in England with no centre to the whole or an attempt at one.'

I may be way off the mark, but I imagine Pevsner as an intense, brooding, patronising intellectual type, and personally I feel it was an urban tragedy we had to put up with him fopping around the streets of Stoke-on-Trent at a time when people were rather more worried about their jobs than whether the neo-industrial skyline juxtaposed in poignant and moving contrast to Methodist austerity and almost Nordic cubic modernism. I can't help hoping some pissed-off, pissed-up, jobless Stokie nicked his camera, gave him a small slap and sent him snivelling across the border to Cheshire.

Actually, I've just Googled Pevsner and he looks as if he was a bit of a dude, so I take it all back.

Yes, Stoke-on-Trent has been through some rough times, and we're not out of the woods by a long chalk; and yes, our club may not be playing sexy football. But I'm sick of my team being bad-mouthed by people who have hardly warmed a seat at the Britannia Stadium, and I'm sick of my city being insulted by ill-informed amateurs and inaccurate reporting.

Ultimately, Priestley found the Potteries fascinating and strangely exotic, while Jones's life is enriched by the friendliness and honesty of the people. I think what I'm saying is we've been insulted – and ultimately exonerated – by far more erudite minds than the two oafs off *Location, Location, Location*. The club, meanwhile, has been denounced by people much better placed to do so – the fans. But this is shaping up to be a strange old season, and I've got this pleasantly malevolent feeling that come May we might be the ones with the last laugh on our bulging, pink, vice-squeezed faces.

On the Tuesday after *Location, Location, Location* goes out, we play Crystal Palace away.

It's a particular fetish of Tony Pulis's to buy someone and then use him out of position until a) the poor sod demands to be transferred or b) Pulis drops him or sells him because, surprise, surprise, the bloke who has played all his professional career as a striker turns out to be just a bit rubbish on the wing.

A similar thing has happened since we bought Richard Cresswell in from Leeds in August, although in fairness to Cresswell he's done a pretty good job for us stuck out on the left.

Tonight, though, he's back in his natural position as a striker because Mama Sidibe, who has been hacked half to death by Togo fans after playing for Mali in a qualifying game for the African Nations Cup, is understandably indisposed.

It's Palace's first match under new manager Neil Warnock – a man so excruciatingly annoying it is no surprise people have taken the time and trouble to work out that Colin Wanker is an entirely appropriate anagram of his name. Maybe I'm doing Colin a disservice, and his constant ranting at officials is merely good-hearted banter and the fact that players under his control seem to collapse to the ground every other minute as if they have been smacked full force in the face, Tom and Jerry style, with an oversized, invisible frying pan is pure coincidence. Even so, I wouldn't be anywhere near the front of the queue for *An Evening With Neil Warnock*, which is the offer apparently being touted to Palace fans on the TV system in the ground. It's a tough sell, possibly on a par with *A Morning With Herpes* or *An Afternoon With Bipolar Disorder*.

Just after half-time, Cresswell slips his marker and heads home a free kick, but two minutes later Palace are level and it looks like we might have pressed the well-worn self-destruct button.

Seven minutes later, though and Cresswell smacks in the rebound after Lawrence hits the post – a true striker's goal. And it's all over bar the shouting when Shawcross makes it 3-1 on seventy-three minutes.

We're fifth in the table and, the day after the Palace game, Channel 4 issues an official apology for the absurd proclamations regurgitated on its programme. Lovely.

CHAPTER 8

Football has almost as much potential for humiliation as childhood. You always know someone who supports the team that thrashes you on the Saturday and inevitably they will surface within forty-eight hours of the final whistle. As far as I remember, I spent most of my first twenty-five years in an almost permanent state of blushing embarrassment, although I was probably no more self-conscious than the next kid. Thankfully, being a Stoke fan over the same period may not always have been a barrel of laughs, but it hasn't been the constant awkward mortification of adolescence.

In any case, losing local derbies or letting in eight in the cup are infinitely preferable (and much less profoundly psychologically damaging) than having to wear your sisters' clothes, even if you are mercilessly ribbed by opposing fans at work for a couple of days afterwards. I remember a particularly hideous pair of purple woolen flares that I inherited from Karen, although to call them flares doesn't really do them justice. They were so wide at the bottom, if I bent my knees slightly, both my feet disappeared under rich folds of deep pink material. And they were so distressingly bright they could be seen from miles around, attracting every kid from a three-mile radius like a beacon of tastelessness to stand in circles laughing at me and making me repeat the shoe disappearing trick over and over again. My mum and dad, thank God, stopped short of making me wear Karen's dresses, although it was probably a close call.

Incidentally, it was another fashion disaster which made me realise I actually *was* bothered what girls thought about me. I had returned from a more-than-usually unsuccessful shoe-shopping trip with my dad when I was maybe nine or ten with a pair of trainers with the alphabet around the bottom and 'left' and 'right' emblazoned in red on the rubber toe-caps. I knew they were too young for me, but I couldn't think of a decent excuse not to wear them until it was too late. Later that day, at the rope swing in the woods, one of the older girls took the mick and I felt a hot, sweaty wave of humiliation slip down my face – a hundred times more uncomfortable than if a boy had ribbed me.

Having said all that, and with the proviso that supporting a crap team will never be as damaging to your self-esteem as sporting a crap pair of your sister's purple flares, this season has started to feel as if there could be plenty of embarrassment along the way, no matter where we end up.

After the satisfaction of beating Palace instilled such bullish optimism in me, we lose at Bristol City, but the following week sees central defender Leon Cort arrive on loan from Crystal Palace and Danny Pugh, who can play on the left side of midfield or defence, comes in on loan from Preston. Cort is certainly a cut above the average Championship defender (although, in fairness, so was Clint Hill, who has gone in the opposite direction from Stoke to Palace) and Pugh is highly rated, although I don't really know anything about him.

So there's a positive buzz around the stadium before the home game against Coventry. Okay, we were all a bit surprised at the lack of transfer activity before the start of the season, but maybe now we have got some quality loan players in who will stop us leaking goals and help turn defence into attack. Typically, though, we're a complete shambles and lose 3-1. Coventry are so much slicker than us, we end up like a bunch of schoolboys chasing the ball. The fact that we've now let in seven goals in our last two home games can't be unconnected to the fact that already this season we've used eleven different players in defence. Patience is beginning to run out, and the new arrivals have only partially averted growing unrest in the stands. After the game, Leon Cort says he's happy to be at Stoke, but it's possible he has his fingers crossed behind his back.

The mood is briefly lightened mid-week when we win 3-2 away at Scunthorpe after going 2-1 down in the 85th minute, but the following Saturday we're all left scratching our heads again, none the wiser about whether this team is close to the worst we have ever seen or two players and a slice of luck away from being one of the best, whether the manager is a commercial and tactical genius or the village idiot or whether spending time and money coming to watch Stoke City is an act of lunacy or the best investment in town.

We lose 1-0 to Sheffield United – the third home defeat in a row – but we actually play much better than of late. I'm infuriated to hear their manager, Bryan Robson, bleat on about us being a one-dimensional long-ball side. Recently Robson has been trying to convince Blades fans that the reason they've been pretty bloody useless since he took over as manager is that the players are in a period of transition because he is teaching them how to play beautiful, sexy football.

There's not much evidence of a budding footballing master race when they play us, though, and his comments smack of someone trying to cling on to his job by keeping the fans onside.

So I'd still rather see us lose to Sheffield United at home rather than, say, wear my sister's flares, but by the time I get home, Robson's comments have left me seething.

To: The Carbon Trust
Dear Sir/Madam,
Have you ever been potholing?
If you have, you will undoubtedly have had to use one of those head torches beloved of sewer workers and safecrackers. I was given one of these gizmos

for Christmas last year to use with the mountain bike I got for my fortieth birthday. The bike (stay with me, I'll get to the point soon) was part of my plan to shift some weight and ride around on a cool-looking piece of kit. At the very least, I thought, I could get one of those rubber all-in-one cycling suits which would hold in my gut and flatten the mannery glands. I even toyed with the idea of having a special one made, like in the Batman films, with a ready-moulded six-pack and pecs. You may not be surprised to hear the bike has been in the shed ever since, and my body has continued its journey floorwards.

Fortunately (and here's the point) my head torch still works, although I would have expected the batteries to have leaked that horrible white goo a long time ago through age and lack of use. I say fortunately (and this really is the point) because last week my wife told me my old trainers (the ones I use for gardening and decorating) were at the back of the wardrobe. Could I find them? Could I buggery, and let me tell you why.

A few months ago (and I swear to God this finally *is* the point) in a laudable attempt to do our bit for Mother Earth, we exchanged our evil, planet-destroying, normal light bulbs for those energy-saving ones. The packet assured me each one would give about the same amount of light as a traditional sixty watt lamp. My arse, they do. I'm no physicist, but I'm almost certain the last time I went searching for my gardening shoes I didn't have to dress up like a miner to find them. Initially, I considered the possibility I had blotted out any similar previous experiences as a psychological self-defence mechanism, such is my dislike of gardening, but then why would I remember this instance? And don't tell me I need to let them warm up for a minute or two. I've sat there for half an hour and the luminescence has gradually changed from 'my God I can't see, someone call an ambulance – I've gone blind' through 'I'm sure that's the phone I can just about make out over there' to the almost blinding 'okay, it's probably safe to start making my way across the room now as long as I keep tapping in front of me with this stick.'

Of *course* they save energy – they don't use any. All I want is to reduce my carbon footprint like a good citizen of the global village, but all I've managed to do is practically break my carbon foot on my son's Tonka Fire Rescue, which was parked up in a particularly gloomy part of the bedroom.

Has anyone calculated the real environmental impact of these so-called energy-saving devices? Firstly there's all the extra bin lorry journeys as millions of people change from Satan's bulbs to ones which don't emit any light; then there's all the extra landfill to put the discarded bulbs in; and to cap it all, there's the additional manufacturing and extra journeys to the shops as people go and buy a second batch of energy-saving lamps in the belief that the first lot must have been faulty. That's not even to mention the energy used keeping up with surging demand for head torches, the disposal of environmentally-lethal batteries and the additional fuel used by ambulances careering all over the country to deal with people who've fallen down the stairs or sliced off their fingers in the eternal dusk in which we are now all forced to live. I think the public should be told.

I'm not sure why I've written this pompous email, or what I'm expecting you to tell me, I just thought I'd get it off my chest. It's been a bad week.
Kind Regards,
David Johnson

PS To show I take my environmental responsibilities seriously, here are a few energy-saving ideas which you're welcome to use and claim as your own.

Persuade everyone to trade in their cars for new energy-saving vehicles – cars that don't go anywhere because they haven't got an engine.

Force airline companies to swap their gas-guzzling jumbos for planes with fuel tanks so small they run out of juice before they get up enough speed to leave the ground.

Light bulbs that don't emit light. Oh, hang on; you've already done that one. My mistake.

CHAPTER 9

It's getting on to the back end of November, and by now the sound of lazy journalists from towns with almost as little as ours going for them sniping at our team is a constant background snigger.

The Britannia Stadium is labelled 'Land of the Giants', reflecting the number of six-foot-two-plus players we have, but also hinting that such players are incapable of producing decent, attractive football. Don't get me wrong, we pretty much *are* incapable of producing decent, attractive football, but the never-ending snide carping from hacks cutting and pasting their opinions from each other is starting to grate.

If they've seen one of our good games, more generous commentators call our football 'route one' or 'direct', while anyone unlucky enough to sit through a bad game – including many of our own supporters – is more likely to describe our tactics as 'hoofing it up front' and the experience as 'akin to drowning in liquid boredom'.

When we drew at West Brom in October, the *Birmingham Evening Mail* wrote: 'At the family dining table, Stoke City would be that unattractive, dysfunctional cousin who sits in the corner, shouting loudly and generally offending everyone. He is socially inept, has no manners and he's a time waster.

'Worst of all, while the rest bring fine wines, he brings a bottle of cheap, nasty plonk. The rest of the family deserve better, as we saw with Albion at the Hawthorns.'

Earlier, during the home game against Plymouth, the away fans deliriously cried 'HOOF!' every time we wellied the ball up front, and they celebrated the fact their team offloaded Pulis to us by singing 'We're not boring any more.'

This Saturday it was Burnley away, and it's a 0-0 thriller which sets off the usual Pavlovian media response.

The *Burnley Citizen* says after the game: 'Big, physical and workmanlike, Stoke City epitomised everything that is wrong with the second tier of the national game. Dull, dour pragmatists, the Potters are anti-football.'

Watching Stoke isn't exactly a Brazilian-style footballing fiesta, admittedly, but neither are we as bad or as cynical as all the kneejerk reporting suggests.

Having said that, after the Burnley game we're tenth in the table and heading south quicker than Vincent Pericard's step-dad can drive. We had an unexpectedly decent start to the season, but we're at risk of drifting into a mid-season crisis in the run-up to the critical Christmas period.

I consider having one of my own fairly regular mid-life crises in sympathy, but I decide I can't afford it at the moment. Stoke have about seven thousand five hundred season ticket holders, and I calculate if all of them buy this book I will make about £7.30. If you take out those who don't read books, those who don't want to read this particular book, those who are incapable of reading and those who will borrow a copy from their mate, I will be pleased to clear seventeen pence. Certainly a long way off a sports car, boat, designer drugs, a diamond-encrusted collar for my pet panther, crates of vintage champagne in which to bathe, gold-digging twenty-one-year-old blondes or any other accessory required for a spectacular tilt at post-forty self-destruction.

Some of the people I still know from school are a disgrace to the whole glorious concept of mid-life crises.

Two of them – and I can feel myself blushing for them as I write this – have taken up horse-riding. I kid you not; bloody horse-riding. What would Jack Nicholson say? What would Keith Richards say? 'Bloody pathetic', that's what they'd say.

In fairness to Lee, another of my contemporaries, at least he had the right idea. Last year he signed up to a fast-track motorcycle training school, learnt to ride a bike which was limited to 70mph and capable of one to sixty in a few days, passed his test and promptly bought a Kawasaki 750. Within a fortnight he was in the hospital with a leg broken in so many places he came out weeks later with the limb in so much scaffolding it was almost all he could do to stop Polish construction workers swarming all over him.

A motorbike crash, of course, has great potential in the mid-life crisis stakes. Unfortunately for Lee, he was pottering around at about thirty, before hitting a bit of gravel, wobbling slightly campily and keeling over with the bike on top of him – all of which, naturally, loses him points.

Someone who works at the hospital tells me they have a special name for mid-life Sunday bikers: donors, which seems to sum it up pretty well. Biking hasn't been a genuine contender for a proper mid-life crisis for years, anyway. From what I can gather it involves dressing up as a Mutant Ninja Turtle every Sunday, setting off with a load of other Mutant Ninja Turtles towards a country pub, stopping to scrape up those who've just passed their tests, starting out for the pub again, arriving at the pub, standing in a circle drinking Britvic 55s and jizzing off over each other's Sperminator 1000s, Dominatrix 900s and Smallpeniscomplex 1100s. It all sounds a bit too public school homo erotic ritual for me.

CHAPTER 10

It's strange what you find to talk about when you have to sit through Stoke City at home to Queens Park Rangers on a Tuesday night.

Ash comes up with an ingenious idea to beat football violence in grounds. As soon as trouble kicks off, the security manager should start playing *The Birdie Song* over the public address system – the theory being that the 1981 novelty number two (in more ways than one) from The Tweets would be too foolish a soundtrack for even coke-fuelled teenagers to carry on scrapping.

Football violence seems to be a pretty embarrassing parody of itself these days. I'd like to say that's a good thing, but I'm not sure I'd mean it. I'm not saying I condone idiots kicking the crap out of each other; it's just that when my dad started taking me to the match in the seventies they did it properly. Maybe it was just because I was small, but even minor rucks seemed to be riots of Tiananmen Square proportions. I remember one of the first games I went to was a 3-2 victory at home against Leeds.

As I, my dad and my sister made our way towards the exit I could hear this strange musical clanging, as if someone was taking down scaffolding in a cave far away. Turns out it was Leeds fans hurling bricks and scrap metal into the exits of the Butler Street paddock. My dad told us we may have to wait a few minutes, but it seemed like hours before we were given the all clear. I can't recall Stoke-on-Trent's brave boys in blue charging over the horizon like the Seventh Cavalry, so I'm guessing we just had to wait for the Leeds nutters to run out of masonry before we could make our escape. I imagine them traipsing off, dejected, like knuckle-dragging zombies from some B-movie.

I can't remember if it was at the same game, but it was around this time my sister gained huge kudos amongst the Stoke City 'bovver boys' – the name given in the '70s and early '80s to football fans with a penchant for extreme violence meted out with Doc Marten boots. We were all coming out of the paddock and my sister was wearing hiking boots – undoubtedly at the insistence of my dad, who as I may have mentioned had a deservedly fearsome reputation for dressing us in the most practical yet embarrassing footwear. As we were about to leave the ground, a group of hoolies ran past us to get at some enemy real or imagined and one particularly ferocious-looking headcase stopped in his tracks, pointed at Karen's feet and said with reverence: 'Look, that girl's got bovver boots on!'

My maths teacher also had suggestions as to how to beat the deep-rooted problem of organised football violence in the early 1980s, although on reflection it's slightly alarming it ever came up as a topic of conversation in between equations and calculating the angles of a triangle.

He was a nice bloke, but a strange-looking fellow, with lots of wiry curly hair and a big beard. His hands were also covered in springy-looking layers of fur – including most of the palms – and I imagine if he was stark bollock naked the only bit of skin you would see would be the two-inch strip containing his eyes between the top of his cheeks and the bottom of his eyebrows. We called him Captain Caveman, although I'm pretty sure that wasn't his real name.

Anyway, Captain Caveman said if fans wanted to fight they should be allowed to fight. Anyone wanting a bit of fisticuffs would be encouraged to stay after the game before being herded into one of the pens in the paddock where they could beat each other to a pulp at leisure. If there was a lull in the action, someone would chuck a copper's helmet in to froth everyone up to a murderous rage again. His eyes would twinkle with mirth as he expounded his theory, although it could just have been a slight hair allergy I suppose.

Some of the players over here from Africa must dampen their boxers in mirth when we agonise over the underlying current of violence surrounding football games. Last month our goal-shy striker Mama Sidibe played for Mali in an African Cup of Nations qualifier victory against Togo, although it almost goes without saying they triumphed without the aid of a goal from the Stoke striker. As Mali fans poured onto the pitch as the final whistle went, the players presumed they were celebrating the win. They were, in fact, being pursued by Togo fans wielding a variety of weapons, including sticks and machetes. In the bloody chaos that followed, Big Mama was set upon and only made it to the tunnel because someone pushed him through a broken window at the side. He was losing a lot of blood from severed veins and slipping in and out of consciousness. Eventually he was bundled into an ambulance, but it was attacked and the driver and medic badly beaten, so Mama was hauled back to the dressing room. Another ambulance was called, and even though this one was an army vehicle, it was still attacked. Eventually Mama got to the hospital where the bleeding was stopped and he was operated on.

Having said that, he hasn't scored a single goal for us this season, so there's only so much sympathy you can have.

But it does make me think it would be worth a few grand to fund a group of Togo fans to come over and sort out our Armani Jeans boys. I can just see their faces as a mob of machete-waving Africans steams down Campbell Road after them, preferably singing some close harmony warrior songs as they plough through the hundreds of Burberry caps dislodged in the hasty retreat.

Given its connections to organised violence, disorganised violence and, at times, extreme right-wing politics, it's difficult to imagine football as a force for good. But, like all great religions, football both divides and unites. A few years ago I went to the Oldham away game which was just a few days after a series of racially-motivated disturbances in towns with significant Asian communities, including Stoke-on-Trent and Oldham.

The police were afraid far-right agitators would hijack the game and use it as an excuse for trouble, and there were certainly reports of clashes between groups of football fans – from both Stoke and Oldham – and Asian youths, but I don't know how true or exaggerated they were. I can't remember much about the game itself, but shortly after kick-off, a group at the back of our end started singing: 'Town full of Pakis, you're just a town full of Pakis,' and it spread until it seemed about half of the Stoke fans were joining in.

I sat there, probably like a lot of us, feeling physically sick, partly out of anger and sadness and partly out of shame for not having the balls to tell the people singing around me to shut the fuck up. Some of the Oldham fans, or at least people in their part of the ground, applauded and joined in with: 'Town full of Pakis, we're just a town full of Pakis.'

I certainly don't think Stoke have a large following of racist fans (the city's enthusiasm for voting in British National Party councillors is more to do with crap wages and an intense distrust of mainstream politicians than skin colour) any more than Oldham do, or Liverpool or Spurs or Swindon. But football can certainly be a vehicle for conflict, whether it's the more traditional scrapping between rival clubs or the rarer, cyclical involvement of the far right.

Albert Camus, that probably never-to-be-repeated combination of intellectual, Nobel Prize-winning author, philosopher and goalkeeper, said: 'What I know most surely about morality and the duty of man I owe to sport.' It's often misquoted with 'sport' replaced by 'football', maybe because football, especially modern professional football, throws up more moral dilemmas than any other sport – if only because it is watched by so many more people than other games. Should I say anything to that bloke with the 'I Drink Blood' tattoo about singing 'town full of Pakis?'

Should I care if we win a penalty with an embarrassing dive? Is the money in the game really obscene? Should I really be singing 'Neil Warnock, you're a wanker, you're a wanker' to a man who, in his private life, may be an extremely pleasant man who helps old ladies across the road and gives thousands of pounds to charities under an assumed name? The answer to the last question, of course, is a resounding 'yes', but the other dilemmas are a bit trickier.

But football is a powerful force for unity as well. Away from the partisan atmosphere of the match, when you meet someone who's a genuine football fan, you instinctively know you share fundamental similarities, regardless of what town or country they're from, how rich or poor they are or what colour their skin is. It's impossible to exaggerate how important this unquestioning acceptance that under the surface we're all basically the same could be. Being a football fan gives thousands – millions – of people who would otherwise be lonely a family and a community.

And watching professional football is just the merest hint of the tip of the iceberg, although attendances are likely to be almost forty million at English league grounds this season. Seven million people play the game in England – almost four million of them are children and more than one million are girls.

There are one hundred and twenty-five thousand teams playing in more than 1,700 affiliated leagues, there are two hundred and seventy football clubs for disabled people with more than ten thousand players and more than four hundred thousand volunteers help to run the game. And remember these are just the figures for *England*. Imagine how mind-boggling they would become if you could collect this sort of information globally and ask yourself how something so popular in almost every country of the world can be anything except a unifying force for good.

Sorry about that. The mind tends to wander alarmingly when the game's about as interesting as a documentary on knitwear. It's still Stoke 0, QPR 0, and next there is an argument about who is the best sleuth on daytime telly. Andy plumps for Columbo because he smokes and therefore must be pretty hard, even though it's only cigars, and no-one would want to get too close to him anyway in case they touched his shabby, greasy mac.

I make what I feel is a strong case for the interfering do-gooder from *Murder, She Wrote* based on a feeling that the old crone is really quite an evil piece of work and that she'd stick a knitting needle in your nads as soon as look at you.

Ash and Andy laugh in my face, though, claiming that even Doctor Sloan, that silver-haired wimp from *Diagnosis: Murder* could kick Jessica Fletcher's wrinkly arse. Ash says Ironside would take the lot of them because of his upper body strength and because, in these politically correct times, no-one would want to beat up a bloke in a wheelchair.

There then follows an argument about whether the rules mean the fights would take place in the present day or in the seventies or eighties, the real heyday of the daytime cop and when there were proper detectives like Dirty Harry, who probably wouldn't think twice about tipping someone out of a wheelchair and stomping on his head.

I realise the conversation has become so boring I might as well concentrate on the football again.

Thirty seconds later I realise my mistake and join in a debate about whether it would be morally wrong to install two-way mirrors in the ladies' changing rooms if you ran a department store. I'm not sure, but I think we decided it would be okay if you were the owner, but it would be going too far if you were just the manager.

As usual in these situations, when nearly everyone in the ground realises there's almost no chance of seeing anything interesting on the pitch, the need to make your own fun transcends the usual barriers between nearby groups and cliques.

'Get him in the book!' Andy shouts after a poor challenge by a QPR player.

'Send him off!' shouts someone about twenty yards away.

'Burn him!' cries Ash.

'Stone him!' the bloke who sits a couple of seats away from us calls.

'The plank! The plank! Make him walk the plank!' someone towards the back shouts.

And so on. Like I say, sometimes you make your own fun.

Inevitably, talk turns to how we could make Stoke matches more exciting and we come up with Nicotine Knockout. All twenty-two players would be kitted out with those criss-crossed ammunition belts beloved of Mexican bandits, but they would be filled with full-strength cigarettes instead of bullets.

Just before kick-off, the ref would light each player a fag and all twenty-two would have to smoke until the half-time whistle goes. Lighters would be banned, and anyone caught not smoking would be sent off. Players would therefore have to chain-smoke, sparking up one cigarette from the stub of another, even if they were racing in for a one-on-one with the keeper.

Ash says it would be even more exciting and unpredictable if a sizeable percentage of the cigarettes were spiked with super-strength marijuana, but we tell him he's being stupid and taking a perfectly sensible idea too far, and anyway what sort of message would that send out to young fans? These players are meant to be role models, for God's sake.

Before you know it, the game's over and somehow we've won 3-1, although there was no danger of St John Ambulance having to draft in reinforcements to cope with the number of people keeling over with excitement-induced strokes.

But hey, we're eighth in the league and that nagging little scratching at the back of my mind that something momentous yet undefined is going on this season just won't go away.

A few days later and we're at home again, this time to Norwich.

We're 1-0 down after five minutes, but somehow almost straight away you know we're going to fight back. We're abysmal for the rest of the first half, then in the opening minutes of the second, Leon Cort equalises. We completely dominate from that moment and end up having sixteen attempts on goal compared to Norwich's eight. Chance after chance goes begging, but even as the clock on the electronic scoreboard shows eighty minutes, eighty-five, eighty-seven, we all seem pretty relaxed, and on eighty-nine, Cresswell swivels and buries the winner, sending another team with a reputation for playing attractive football away with nothing.

After the match, Glenn Roeder, Norwich's manager, predictably calls us nothing more than a long-ball side and their fanzine, *Cheep Shot*, says we play 'some of the most direct and cynical football in the league'. And up to a point they're right, but somehow this game feels like a turning point; as if the players and the manager and the fans have had enough of the booing and the bickering and the snooty sniping from people who haven't really got a clue about our club.

It's the night of the works' Christmas party, and I miss the start of the Sheffield United away game on the radio because I'm bathing Harry. By the time I'm in the car we're 2-0 up.

Twenty-five minutes into the game, as Alison drops me off at the casino where we're having the do, we're three up and it's all over bar the shouting.

I get myself over-excited by this delirious thrashing of a team widely expected to be promoted back to the top flight this season and throw myself exuberantly into a downing-gin-and-tonics-in-one bonding session with the boss.

I try my best, but really pressing the self-destruct button at works' dos, rather like being able to turn the pages of a newspaper without licking my fingers, seems to be yet another thing I find impossible to do since I turned forty. Gone are the warrior days of my twenties when I would not even be on nodding terms with my sanity by 11pm and I would wake up on my desk at work to find myself completely naked and my P45 tied with a piece of tinsel to my flaccid member. Instead, I'm in the taxi and on my way home before midnight.

But I don't really care. I'm nicely drunk, in ten minutes I'll be leaning over my little boy's cot listening to him snoring gently and we're up to fifth in the league. And at least I haven't got to the stage of wanting to take up bloody horse-riding or crashing my Menopausa 1200 into a tree just yet.

Quote of the week: 'I thought the lads looked lively and confident before the first goal went in.' That was Bryan Robson, Sheffield United's manager. We scored after ninety seconds.

CHAPTER 11

Alison finds an empty bottle of whisky in the drinks cabinet, and she accuses me of being an alcoholic. It just confirms her suspicions after I came home the other night smelling of gin, and she seems to think I'm pouring it on my cornflakes or feverishly necking it with trembling, desperate hands while I've got Harry strapped in his high chair for his breakfast.

'Don't tell your mum, son, it's our little secret. Just a little steadier before I go to work. What's the harm, eh, lad? Here, have a swig of this.'

I suggest that alcoholics, like all addicts, are fiendishly cunning and masters of disguising their problem, even from those closest to them. It seems pretty unlikely, therefore (I argue), that any dipsomaniac worth his salt would polish off a bottle of Jura's finest, smack his lips and then attempt to hide the empty bottle in the drinks cabinet.

'You're obviously a very stupid alcoholic, then,' she says.

Offended, I tell her I might be double-bluffing and casually leaving the evidence for her to find so she thinks it must be some sort of innocent mistake, but I sense this isn't really helping my cause.

Still thinking of all the rapier-sharp put-downs I should have come out with I set off for work on the day of the Watford game.

I'm running a bit late. Not massively late – the sort of late where it becomes funny because there is absolutely no chance of getting where you want to go on time – but that horrible, stressful, naggingly anxious sort of late where, with a fair wind and a sprint up the boss's blind side, you might get away with it.

My mood isn't brightened when, a few hundred yards out of the house I have to slam the brakes on behind a car travelling just a fraction quicker than I can walk. There's nowhere to overtake for more than two miles, and I scan the car's windows for evidence. My heart sinks.

There it is, bottom left – the Curse Of The Oak Twig. If you ever find yourself stuck behind a car with a National Trust sticker in the window, you might as well kick back, put something mellow on the CD and relax, because no matter how vital your appointment, you haven't got a prayer of arriving on time.

If the car you are following has a National Trust sticker and one of those unaccountably annoying A Dog Is For Life stickers then you would be advised to pull over at the earliest opportunity, get out, gather your belongings and walk. You'll pass the car about thirty yards down the road.

If the car you are following has a National Trust sticker, an unaccountably annoying A Dog Is For Life sticker and one of those slightly unnerving Christian fish symbols (you know the one, the one that might as well say 'I'm one step away from joining the Jesus-Is-An-Alien-And-He-Has-Told-Me-We-Must-All-Kill-Ourselves-Or-At-Least-That's-What-You've-Got-To-Do-After-You've-Given-Me-All-Your-Money-And-I've-Slept-With-Your-Wife-And-Your-Daughter-Brotherhood) then you may indeed as well take your own life because you ain't going anywhere.

The Corolla I'm following has two out of the three (Curse Of The Oak Twig and Suicide Cult) and I realise I'm doomed.

I get to the office late and start my usual preparations for a Stoke match at work, logging on to the Radio Stoke website and finding the page with the live text commentary. Today's slightly different, though, because the game's on telly, so I find the pair of binoculars Rich keeps in his desk especially for these occasions when you need to see the office TV set sixty yards away.

Text commentary is quite possibly the weirdest and most unsatisfying way of following a match I have ever come across. (If you're interested, the second most unsatisfying way, on a bad day, is to be at the Britannia Stadium, cursing the time, emotion and money you have invested.) Every minute or two someone (I presume it hasn't been automated yet, although it certainly reads as if it's been written by a computer) types in the highlights since the last update and presses return. Probably because they haven't got time, they make absolutely no attempt to inject any excitement into the proceedings (mind you, you could say the same about a significant proportion of the Stoke players on occasions) and the result is a bizarre, stilted list of almost meaningless descriptions.

61. Goal kick (Simonsen) resulting in open play.
64. Attacking throw cleared by Shawcross (infield) to Fuller (offside).
65. Free kick cleared by Shawcross (infield) to Fuller (offside).
67. Long ball by Lawrence (right channel) to Fuller (offside).
68. So dull. Can't take any more. Tell Carol I love her. Kiss kids for me. Gun to temple (right side).
69.
70.
71.

It's a distinctly awkward task trying to keep a handle on the game, what with the phones going, the shooting neck pains from keeping the binos trained on the distant TV set and the live text commentary bloke doing himself in.

But we get a 0-0 draw against the team who are top of the table.

Stephen Wright gets a boot in the head and gets carried

off late in the game. He tells *The Sentinel*: 'I should have had thirteen stitches, but I told them I wanted fourteen. I'm not superstitious, but I'm not having thirteen.'

Call me a traditionalist, Stephen, but that sounds pretty superstitious to me. It's one of the few interesting things to happen in a game that does little to change the prevailing view that Stoke are a long-ball side, and of course it's on telly, so all the knockers will feel smugly vindicated.

This is what the *Sunday Mirror* says: 'Thrill-seekers in the Potteries who expected fine art to rival a Wedgwood dinner service were short-changed by a game with all the charm and subtlety of a breeze-block. In fairness, Stoke – fit, functional and utterly one-dimensional – probably deserved to win, if only because Richard Lee produced excellent saves when creativity threatened to gatecrash the tedium.'

To say it's not a classic would be like saying it's a bit fresh in Antarctica, but we're fifth in the table and unbeaten in five games.

I'm listening to the Blackpool away game on the radio. In spite of dominating from the kick-off, we go 1-0 down after fourteen minutes. I wait for the usual almost pleasurable shot of self-pity mixed with a healthy loathing for my own club brought on by the certain knowledge that we have already thrown another game away within a quarter of an hour.

But that was the old Stoke. The feeling never comes and I realise my subconscious has been reprogrammed over the last few games by aliens from the planet Optimisticus. I go to the kitchen, pour some water in a glass and, as suspected, it's half full. It's a strange but not entirely unpleasant sensation for me.

From the minute we go a goal down we absolutely pulverise them. Fuller equalises from a tight angle, and shortly before half-time Cort heads us into the lead. Just after the hour, Fuller, who before today hasn't scored in his last nine appearances, gets his second of the day.

Come six o'clock, West Brom are top, Watford are second, Bristol City are third and we're fourth.

After the game, the aliens from the planet Optimisticus make me celebrate with a few whiskies. Nothing drastic, you understand, and Alison and I start the usual, weary, shuffling, going-to-bed preparations. I decide I could do with just the smallest nightcap, and, because I'm standing right next to the drinks cabinet, I decide it would be a criminal waste of energy to get a glass.

As I tip the bottle back for a small swig I freeze. Alison, who I thought was already upstairs, is standing in the doorway looking at me as if she had caught me relieving myself on the kitchen floor. I explain to her I'm trying to save on the washing up, but I can see she's not having any of it.

Her look says: 'You are a sick man. I love you, but you disgust me and you need help. Without doubt, the reason you have not provided me with a second child is because you have sterilised yourself with strong liquor and I will make you pay.' That's a lot to say with one look, granted, but my wife has a remarkable talent for non-verbal communication. You should see her headbutts.

Oh, how Stoke fans love West Brom. No matter how good they are (and without doubt they are by far the most gifted team in the division), no matter how many millions their squad is worth, no matter how beautiful and pure their style of play, they just can't help but lose to us oiks from a few miles up the M6.

Personally, I pity the West Brom fans, precisely *because* they have been watching so many great games and players over the last few years. Their team is the equivalent of internet porn. It has raised the bar to an unhealthy level. In that age of innocence before the world wide web came along, a reasonable fantasy would involve having sex outdoors or a threesome with your girlfriend and the next-door neighbour's wife.

But we've been ruined. With almost every perversion known to man (or animal) available at the click of a mouse, even our tamest daydreams are more likely to involve twelve cheerleaders, root vegetables and a rubber glove. West Brom fans have had a taste of paradise with their sexy football and their games tumescent with excitement. But when we turn the computer off, we still need to muster up sufficient enthusiasm to make love to our partners, just as Baggies fans, with the cyclical passage of managers, players and styles, will one day once again be faced with missionary football once a week at best.

Since 1988, West Brom have beaten us just once in twenty-three attempts. Admittedly, that's marginally better than my record at trying to take Louise Fisher's virginity (nought out of thirty-seven attempts), but it's still sticking two great big fingers up at the law of averages or the theory that quality will eventually out.

Three days before Christmas we play them at the Brit, and they may as well have left Birmingham gift-wrapped with a big bow and a label reading: 'A gift to the people of the city of Stoke-on-Trent'.

As usual, the Baggies look streets ahead of us, playing quick, fluid passes born out of technical ability coupled with imagination and confidence. But, as usual, it doesn't seem to get them anywhere and within five minutes Fuller finishes crisply to put us one up. Every player is working for his teammates, the crowd is right behind them and we're even stringing some nice football together as Fuller gets his second. The atmosphere is fantastic – wave after wave of noise pouring onto the pitch, almost visibly puffing the players' chests out like some communal kiss of life.

At this moment it is unimaginable that fans ever talked

of boycotting games, that disagreements in the stands could almost turn to violence and that Tony Pulis could criticise the very people who help pay his wages.

At this moment I worship them all. Tony Pulis is the Messiah and I love each and every player to the extent that, should scientific advances allow, I would like to bear each and every one of them a son.

In the sixty-sixth minute Fuller instinctively outwits two defenders as he cuts inside and buries his third into the far corner. The Baggies get one back, but it means nothing and we're never really in trouble.

This is what one of the Birmingham papers says after our efficient annihilation of West Brom.

'Speaking of Christmas presents, one could be mistaken for thinking that Tony Pulis will be finding a table football under his tree tomorrow. It'll be the kind of table football game which has a row of nine defenders lining up across the width of the pitch in front of the eighteen-yard box. If you turn the handle quickly enough you can even get one of the 'players' to launch the ball down the pitch. One could also be mistaken for thinking it's where the Stoke manager takes his inspiration from.'

And later: 'Stoke sat back in large numbers and crudely scrambled balls away for large periods of the second half, a period when Kiely [Albion's keeper] was the only man left in Albion's half of the pitch. An astonishing number of Stoke players also became injured – badly enough to need treatment, but not badly enough to require permanent withdrawal from the game.

'Not surprisingly, Tony Mowbray [Albion's manager] bore the hallmarks of a disillusioned man after the game. He was pleased with his side's effort – if not their defending – but his grimace suggested that he was in despair at the methods used by Stoke to take a victory.

'While there is no right or wrong way to play football,

there is no doubt that there are vulgar methods. And Stoke City are the John Prescott of football – big and as ugly as sin.

'One can only praise Stoke through gritted teeth. It's difficult being complimentary about a side who rely on percentages as much as an accountant and who simply are soiling the game.

'If they achieve promotion then it will be deserved. But at what cost to football as a sport? English football is going through an image crisis right now – it needs Stoke's brand of play like it needs a hole in the head.'

Soiling the game? I can't tell you how much sweeter this pre-meditated, poorly thought-out, whiney moralising makes victory. It's a couple of days away from Christmas, I'll be spending some time with my family, going out drinking with my friends and we're fourth in the table. The next couple of weeks, with three games in quick succession, may well be the tipping point – towards a genuine shot at glory, or back to mid-table nothingness. It could be a vintage Christmas.

CHAPTER 12

And so it turns out – at least in some respects.

Every year I write a Christmas list, compiled from ideas I have throughout the year for gifts that would enrich my life and furnish me with fond memories and interest into my dotage.

It's not that I'm materialistic or greedy, and I agree it's better to give than receive. But if you're *going* to receive, why not receive what you want?

Every year, my wife, who I foolishly entrust to co-ordinate this festive privilege, completely ignores my wishes and steadfastly refuses to pass them on because all my ideas are 'boring'.

In a typical year, my list may be something like this:
Skiing lessons
First series of *Twin Peaks* on DVD
Le Creuset 24cm casserole dish
Thing to attach my iPod to the car stereo
T-shirts
Books
CDs

But on Boxing Day my thank you note list might look something like this:
Facial scrub and moisturiser
Bottle of vintage port
Pasta maker
Trousers
Boxer shorts
Bedside lamps

Now don't get me wrong, I would appreciate all of these items, but *they're not on the list*. In fact I remember I was very excited about the bedside lamps. When we decided we had to move from our tiny house in Penkhull because Alison was pregnant (I mean the house was going to be too small for the two of us and a baby, not that the house was so small we had to move because Alison's growing stomach was getting her wedged in there), pretty much the only stipulation I made was that our bedroom had to be big enough for a double bed with bedside cabinets on each side so we could each have a reading light.

In Penkhull I would read for five minutes and Alison would start huffing and harrumphing and telling me the light was keeping her awake. But with my own personal little reading lamp I could plough through *War and Peace* without disturbing anyone.

Unfortunately, although they looked nice and trendy, the lights I got for Christmas had two key design faults. Firstly they had very narrow shades – so narrow, in fact, you can't get your hand in to press the switchy-on thing without picking the whole shooting match up, turning it upside down with your left hand, smearing KY Jelly on your right hand and forcing it up the shade like a vet delivering a stubborn calf.

The second is they smell of fish. I'm sure there must be a logical explanation, but I'm buggered if I know what it is. As soon as you turn either of them on, an alarmingly powerful piscine odour fills the room, making it impossible to concentrate on *Noddy Goes On Holiday*, let alone *War And Peace*, and turning both of them on leads to complaints from the neighbours and tumbling house prices.

All of which means, of course, we now have a nice big bedroom, with an attractive but useless his and hers lighting system, and I'm still banned from reading.

This year, though, for the first time in a decade, she's cracked under pressure, and the conversion rate from the sacred Christmas list is virtually one hundred per cent.

The only exception is a strange-looking contraption called the Jamie Oliver Flavour Shaker, or some such nonsense, which looks like a plastic Russian doll with a ceramic ball inside. It seems to do the same thing as a pestle and mortar but much less effectively and in twice the amount of time, and the only real use of it appears to be to line the pockets of Mr Oliver himself.

When my sister-in-law Caroline, who kindly bought me the gadget, asks me what I think, I make the crucial mistake of telling the truth. My wife calls me an ungrateful arse, but I prefer to think of it as a valuable lesson about the dangers of going off-list.

Still, it's been a fantastic Christmas – a boozy Christmas Eve with friends on the traditional pub crawl, Christmas Day with my mum and dad, Boxing Day spent sitting on the sofa at Caroline and Ian's as what seems like seven hundred and thirty-four children demolish the house around us – and I decide to give Mr Oliver the benefit of the doubt and hold off putting his ingenious invention on eBay until the New Year. At least it doesn't smell of rotting halibut, which in my book counts for a lot.

I love Christmas, and I look forward to it like a six-year-old, but generally you can rely on Stoke City to be the one blot on the festive landscape, like an unwelcome but ever-present cantankerous, flatulent relative.

We have been in the play-off positions going into the festive period for the last three seasons, but every time we have stumbled between Boxing Day and New Year and gone on to screw it up. In 2004 we were sixth at Christmas, but ended up twelfth at the end of the season, and in 2005 we were fifth, but ended up thirteenth. Last year we were fourth and missed out on the play-offs on the last day of the season to finish eighth.

If 2008 is to be our glory year, we really need to consolidate our position towards the top of the table over the next three games.

I listen to the Boxing Day game away at Barnsley in the car on the way back from my mum and dad's. They live out in the wilds of Shropshire, and the commentary keeps cutting between Radio Stoke and a completely different game on Radio Shropshire. After ten minutes I haven't got a clue what's going on.

It turns out Barnsley go ahead with a penalty and Lawrence equalises on half an hour – again from the penalty spot. In the second half, Barnsley go ahead, but Lawrence makes it 2-2 with six minutes to go. A minute later, just as I'm becoming comfortable with the idea of coming away with one point instead of three, Simmo makes a hash of a high ball and we're losing again.

Deep into injury time, we get a free kick on the edge of the penalty area – surely the last attack of the game. As the ball comes in, the referee blows his whistle, and players and fans alike think it's the end of the game. But he's given us a second penalty, God knows why, and Liam Lawrence gets his hat-trick with the final kick of the match.

It's only a point, but we're up to third.

A couple of days later we play Plymouth away. Pulis has lost patience with Simmo's vulnerability on crosses and he gives Russell Hoult his league debut after joining us nearly a year ago. In true Stoke fashion, Hoult manages to get himself sent off and banned for the next three matches. We draw 2-2 and slip to fourth.

Hull at home is an awful affair, and we certainly don't deserve more than the point we get. Fuller has gone back to Jamaica for his grandmother's funeral and we really miss him. Hardly surprising when you consider our strike force for the day is Mama Sidibe, a centre forward who halfway through the season has yet to score, and

Jon Parkin, a man who, let's be frank, wobbles when he walks.

The highlight of an extremely dull day is the Hull fans serenading Parkin with: 'Get your tits out, get your tits out, geeeet your tits out for the lads!' Marvellous.

CHAPTER 13

Back at work, all the girls have started the traditional January diets and they spend the entire day working out how many points the purple Quality Street is, or if they can still get hammered drinking neat vodka instead of wine. Some of them have even got handy cardboard ready reckoners which they whip out in the canteen, holding everyone else up in the queue and becoming increasingly frustrated because they can't work out how to use the patented Blubber-b-Gone Calorie Calculator Wheel.

As the afternoon wears on, and the Christmas chocolate begins to leave their system, they become first slightly testy, then downright rude, and by 5 p.m. there are sporadic outbreaks of random violence in the office. The atmosphere is getting so ugly I suggest we should introduce Swearwatchers, with everyone allocated twenty swear points a day.

A 'bloody' would be one point, while a 'twat' would be five and a 'fuck' would be seven. You could have two 'shits' on a green day and five 'craps' on a red day, but a 'wank' would be completely out of the question unless you traded it for at least three 'cock-ends'. The idea isn't universally popular, and they're starting to get that look you see on crocodiles just before they launch themselves at some big-eyed wildebeest calf so I beat a hasty retreat.

I decide to go for Plan B – a multi-million-selling diet plan which will enable me to give up work and sit in cafés all day drinking lattes with JK Rowling discussing how all our hard-earned wealth has not brought us true happiness.

My book will be just a fraction of a page long and consist of nine words: 'Eat a bit less. Move around a bit more.' There would then be a couple of hundred blank pages for people to record their amazing escape from morbid obesity.

Deep down I know it's not going to work. People don't take kindly to being told they are overweight because they are greedy and lazy. We would rather kid ourselves that eating lentils on a Thursday will miraculously dispel fat if we face south and add puréed goat hair to our meals on a waning moon.

You'd think it was a simply-enough grasped equation: burn off more calories than we shove down our throats and we'll lose weight; deep throat cream eclairs and do no exercise and we'll be shoehorning our fat arses and undulating thighs into stretchy leisurewear in no time. No matter, we still expect to see globules of rancid, melting blubber dribble from every crevice after the first half hour of following the latest fad diet as long as it's endorsed by some vapid, air-brushed, bulimic celeb.

Let's face it – these celebrities have so much money and time on their hands and are so adrift from reality they would happily snort dog faeces if a woman in a white coat and with a qualification from Argos told them it would shrink their saddlebags. Ignore them. They're insane.

I'm on an early shift and the air is painfully cold as I close the door behind me. I usually hate this feeling, having to force myself out of the luxurious warmth of our bed and leaving for work without seeing Harry. But it's a beautiful dawn, the air filled with snow particles so tiny they rise as well as fall, picked out like tiny specks of glitter in the outside light. There's a cartoon perfect crescent moon stuck on the blue-grey sky, a peachy-pink glow growing behind the Britannia Stadium and long, sweeping horse-tail clouds above it.

I'm starting to get excited about the FA Cup tie coming up against Newcastle. It's a different kind of feeling than the anticipation of a league match – there's no real apprehension because I'm really not that bothered if we win or lose. But it's always great to draw a big club at home – the stadium comes alive and you just know the players are going to punch above their weight, driven on by the big crowd and the desire to prove they can mix it with the Ferrari-driving Premier League bling boys. We play brilliantly, Newcastle are low on confidence and form after a dreadful run, and given a bit of luck we could have won. In the end, it's a 0-0 draw, but every one of our players excels.

In situations like this it often annoys football fans that their players look as if they are trying harder, running faster, jumping higher and caring more than they do in a bog-standard league game. It's probably inevitable, and possibly physical, as extra adrenalin squirts into the system, pumped by the national attention, the extra noise of the crowd and the fear of humiliation. It's fight or flight, and in extreme circumstances a human can perform seemingly superhuman acts. I'm generally a flight sort of guy in these situations, unless you count making it to the bar before the towels go up, but each to their own, I suppose.

There's definitely a widening gap between players and fans, though. Even in the Championship the young men who determine your mood for the rest of the weekend earn five, ten or twenty thousand pounds a week, sponsorship money, one-off payments from transfers and win bonuses. How *can* the people sitting in the stands relate to them? It's impossible, especially as players, perhaps sensing the increasing distance themselves, have almost no face-to-face contact with fans.

It's a shame, because the man sitting with his daughter in the row in front of me and the lads in the Burberry caps in the corner and the bloke in the wheelchair down there and the old dear with a scarf covered in so many metal badges it's a wonder she can lift her head to see the game pay their wages as sure as my boss pays mine. Entrance fees may not even cover players' pay, let alone contribute to the other massive costs involved (Stoke employ about five hundred people on a match day) but almost every penny that comes into the game is attributable to us, the fans. The advertising money, the sponsorship, the money from the television companies, the merchandise sales, the catering, the hospitality; all of it comes about because of the billions of people around the world who watch the game.

It's hardly any wonder the connection between fan and player has been all but severed, when so many stars move on for purely financial gain. A few years ago I saw a documentary following different players. One was a famous Premier League star and he was showing off his Rolex, which he was happy to tell everyone cost £20,000. Then he was in a Ferrari showroom and he said to the offscreen film maker something like: 'Yeah, well, this is why we do it, this is why we do all that training.' I'm sure it must have gone down well with the people who paid £20 or £30 a game to watch him play. They must have wept for the poor little poppet having to train three days a week, play a game of football and pick up his paltry £50,000 pay slip. It's practically slave labour. Even if buying cars costing five times the annual salary of most of the people who pay your wages *is* your chief motivation, imagine being so thick you actually *tell* them.

In one sense, fans get sick of seeing players brazenly siphoning as much money as they can from local factory and office workers who adore them before upping sticks and going to a club which is prepared to let them pick even more from the pockets of their supporters. I feel almost embarrassed for the procession of foreign players who arrive in Britain announcing they want to play in the Premier League because it's the most exciting league in the world. Yeah, right. If the bloke waving the plastic clipboard at arrivals told them there'd been an administrative error and they would, in fact, be paid exactly the same amount as at the club they'd just dropped like a sack of spuds, do you think they'd say:

'That's very disappointing, and I do think it shows a certain lack of professionalism. However, the Premier League is the most exciting league in the world, so take me to the training ground without delay. And after training you can drop me at the offices. Perhaps I can help my desk-bound colleagues develop more robust administrative and financial procedures to prevent this inconvenience happening to someone else'? Not a bloody chance.

It's quite a coincidence that foreign players started fawning about the Premier League being the best in the world at pretty much exactly the same time as Premier League clubs started paying more than anyone else, and the incidences of incoming players getting all misty-eyed with joy as they step off the plane at Heathrow have grown with every season that the gap between wages in the Premier League and those in the rest of Europe has widened still further. The latest figures for the 2006/2007 season show salary increases of thirteen per cent, resulting in the highest wages to revenue ratio since the league began in 1992/1993.

Increasing sales were cancelled out and then some by payments to players, and Premier League wages were seventy-five per cent higher than Spain's La Liga and at least double the total wage costs of Europe's other major leagues. In other words, if the trend continues, expect to see incoming players actually breaking down and blubbering on live television as they tell us how, as a foetus, they dreamed of playing in the Premier League – the most exciting league in the world.

Perhaps managers and chairmen should start slipping truth drugs into the drinks of players looking for a big-money move.

Manager: 'So, Robin, we've had you watched for some time and we like the way you play. Your agent tells us you're looking for a move to the Premier League – looking for the challenge of playing in the most exciting league in the world, I'll be bound.'

Robin Basta: 'No. I don't even really like playing football. I want to turn up late to training, sit on the bench on Saturdays and make more money in a week than I know what to do with. I want to make so much money I can buy a Rolex every morning and throw it in the bin every night. I want diamond-encrusted underpants and I want to adorn my pubic hair with platinum thread. I want to have a Ferrari that runs on vintage champagne and I want to employ someone to brush my teeth for me. Oh, and a Nissan Micra for my mother.'

Manager: 'Interesting. Aren't there any other reasons you want to come and play for us?'

Robin Basta: 'Yes. My friend Ego Massivo plays over here and he says the most beautiful girls in England all want to sleep with footballers – even Peter Crouch gets lucky. I want to go to bed with eight lapdancers, three goats and a chicken and have one of the girls film it all. What's the worst that could happen?'

Manager, head in hands: 'Dear God, what the hell happened to this game?'

Robin Basta: 'Oh, by the way, my agent said to give you this brown envelope stuffed full of euros.'

Manager: 'You're in.'

There's probably an element of chicken and egg here, and some of the money has followed the players rather than the players just following the money, and, quite frankly, I find it hard to get too worked up about the whole subject. People like money, simple as that. It can't really come as a surprise to us that young men who happen to be good at kicking a football around are no different. (And make no mistake, even though we spend a good proportion of each game screaming at players that our nan, who's been dead for ten years, could have won that header, these young men are *really* good at kicking a football around. I once played in a team with a guy who had made one substitute appearance for Leek Town – a team currently on course to be relegated from the Unibond

Premier Division – and he was so much better than the rest of us it was depressing and put an end forever to the sneaking suspicion that the only reason I was working in a succession of jobs that I disliked intensely was because a talent scout hadn't spotted me yet.)

Let's face it, if someone came along and said they'd pay you twice the amount for doing the same job, what would you do? You wouldn't see most of us for dust. I suppose there's an argument to say there must come a point when top players have so much money they will never be anything less than super-rich for the rest of their lives, so surely pursuing more wealth becomes an irrelevance, but that would involve a pretty tough battle against human nature.

I feel sorry for some of these guys who have had such a strange and cosseted existence from the age of sixteen and seventeen, cut adrift from reality until their mid thirties when suddenly there you are with a bulging bank account and a boat but no purpose in life and no-one telling you how brilliant you are. They can't *all* be employed as TV pundits, so if they can't find a niche, what do they do? I'm pretty sure I'd rattle around the Mediterranean for a couple of years before pressing the self-destruct button out of sheer boredom. I used to be one of those who said they would quite happily never work again if their numbers came up, but now I'm not so sure. Sitting around the swanky pools of Europe and the Middle East for the remainder of your days is like deliberately opting out of life – a long, luxurious suicide.

And you know what? We whinge on about how much money there is in the game, how mercenary players and managers are and how it's not like it used to be, but I'm not convinced that, if we're completely honest with ourselves, we're really that bothered. Our attachment to our team isn't really dependent on individual players, even if they're one of the greatest in the history of the game. I'm incredibly proud of my club's connections with Sir Stanley Matthews, but I don't think it affects my fundamental relationship with Stoke City one iota.

So, conversely, why would a succession of mercenary kids out for what they can get affect it? Your connection to your club is much more about where you're from, civic pride, having a laugh with your mates and the sense of belonging to something important and worthwhile – no matter how rubbish your team is.

It's no coincidence we say 'Stoke City are' instead of 'Stoke City is'. If you read reports on football games in US papers or in English language papers produced in many other parts of the world, they will use the grammatically correct: 'Manchester United is top of the English Premier League after a fine victory over Arsenal yesterday', and it grates horribly because it goes against things we instinctively and unconsciously know.

When a Stoke fan says 'Stoke City' or a Liverpool fan says 'Liverpool' or a Bury fan says 'Bury', we don't mean a club in the singular, because we all know a football club is not just a standalone company with its limits defined by who owns it on paper or who sits on the board or what its turnover is. When a fan talks about Stoke City he's including not just the corporation, but also the players and the millions of people from the same city who have invested in it both financially and emotionally over the last one hundred and forty-five years. (Our club was formed in 1863, the same year the formal laws of the game were drawn up, a heritage robust enough to withstand a few mercenaries.)

In a similar way, that's why we say 'we're playing Newcastle next week' rather than 'Stoke are playing Newcastle next week' or '*they* are playing Newcastle next week'. Instinctively we reflect our feelings of belonging to the club, of being a vital part of it and even of possessing it in some way. We *are* the club, the generations of fans who have come through the turnstiles and the generations who have yet to come through the turnstiles. We have a much better claim to ownership of the club or to belonging to it than the ever-changing collections of players who pull on the shirt.

I suppose that's why, as a teenager, my bottom drawer was full of Stoke programmes dating back years, but my wardrobe doors and walls were covered with the pictures of rock stars. I don't think I ever considered cutting pictures of players out of the programmes and sticking them on the walls because, although I wouldn't have formalised the thought process, I realised that the stars I saw on Saturdays were transient and not really the root cause of my passion for Stoke City.

The posturing rockers, on the other hand, were the direct creators, producers and suppliers of the emotional connection I felt to their music and, barring the odd overdose or vomit-choking incident here or there, they tended to be more permanent.

It's good that our reputation for attractive, flowing, cultured football is spreading far and wide. After the draw with Newcastle, the *Northern Echo* says: 'Much has been written about the unrefined nature of Newcastle's football this season, but if the St James' Park faithful are disillusioned with Allardyce's methods, they should try watching Stoke every week.

'The Potters' sole tactic was to lump the ball in the general direction of man-mountain Mama Sidibe, in the hope that the Mali international would knock it in the general direction of the pacy Ricardo Fuller.'

Now I could be wrong, but I'm prepared to bet the reporter from the *Northern Echo* hasn't been watching Stoke every week, and I imagine his boss was livid to learn how much time he'd been spending keeping such a detailed eye on a team several hundred miles away from the paper's readership area.

So it would be great to go to Newcastle for the replay

and knock their Premier League arses out of the cup. Their manager, Sam Allardyce, has been hanging on to his job by the skin of his teeth, and it's almost inevitable that if they lose to lower-league ruffians like us he'll be handed his P45 pronto.

I admit I'm not a good judge of character. Put in charge of recruitment, I would undoubtedly bring the strongest company to its knees in a matter of weeks because of my complete inability to make accurate assessments about potential employees. Unwittingly, I would hire murderers, rapists, loan sharks, stalkers, flashers and estate agents. 'Congratulations, Mr Hitler, when can you start?' I would say. 'But I'm sorry, Mr Branson, you've been unsuccessful on this occasion. You really should reconsider a career in business; you're clearly unsuited to it. And Mr Gates, I hope you take this in the spirit it is given – as advice which I know may be painful to hear now, but which I believe will stand you in good stead for the future: give up on this ridiculous pipedream. The computer will never catch on.'

A girl I went out with for several years turned out to be a lesbian, although how much I contributed to this outcome is open to question, at least by me, if not by everyone else I know who says I'd be enough to put Ulrika Jonsson off blokes. Ash says he must be a lesbian, too, because he can't stop ogling girls' breasts, but I'm not sure that counts.

On many occasions I've refused to talk to someone because they've got a 'mean face', only to find out months later they are hilarious, funny, kind and quite probably on the shortlist for a Nobel Peace Prize. On many others I've made instant friendships with people who later turn out to be complete scumbuckets and who end up telling me about what fun they had when they were a guard at Bergen-Belsen.

I was certain my wife would never look at me twice. Once she did I was certain she would soon realise what an horrendous mistake she'd made and I was certain she would never become unhealthily obsessed with the way dishwashers are loaded. Wrong on all three counts.

When it comes down to it, I'm not even a good judge of my *own* character. I think I'm much funnier than I actually am, I think I'm far more intelligent than I actually am and I have no problem convincing myself that I haven't got man-boobs, I'm just developing more and more defined pecs, even though I haven't done any exercise for months.

What I'm saying is that I'm prepared to accept the possibility that I've got it wrong about Kevin Keegan. Perhaps he isn't the most annoying man in the known universe after all, and I suppose it's even possible my desire – need, almost – to tie him against a tree and kick footballs at him all day long is misplaced. But for the moment I believe he is the vile offspring of Lucifer himself.

Sam Allardyce actually gets sacked a few days before the game with Ipswich in the league on the Saturday, and hopes are high for beating managerless Newcastle in the replay on Wednesday. But just hours before the game, the news comes in that Kevin Keegan has agreed to come out of managerial retirement and take over for the second time at the club where, for reasons beyond me, he is worshipped. Immediately the media go into Keegan frenzy.

Every radio station with a sporting bent talks about nothing else, every satellite sports channel sends three hundred cameras and twenty reporters up to St James' Park. Within ten minutes of the news breaking I have heard the phrases 'King Kev', 'the return of the Messiah' and 'football's not just a game up here, it's a religion' about four hundred and ninety-nine times more than I would have liked throughout my entire life.

By the time the game kicks off, Radio 5 Live is in such a lather about it all, the entire station may as well drop to its collective knees and take Mr Keegan in its collective mouth.

We're doomed, of course, and we get stuffed 4-1. The press

dress it up as a minor miracle brought about by Keegan's awe-inspiring motivational qualities beaming down from the stands above like some sort of celestial gift from the angels on high, but in reality Newcastle are pretty rubbish; it's just that we're considerably worse.

CHAPTER 14

I seem to be going through some sort of death terror phase. I'm acutely conscious of how long menial tasks take and I can't help calculating exactly how much of my remaining time on this planet has been wasted. Picking up my son's wooden blocks, I calculate, is forty-eight seconds I will never be able to reclaim; that flicking through a hundred channels of digital dross on the television is almost an hour gone up in smoke, and the three solid days I've been listening to Newcastle fans droning on about the return of Kevin Keegan on the radio could certainly have been better spent. By sticking my tongue in the electrics, for example, or staring at a wall.

We all get a bit weird occasionally, I suppose, so I can't blame King Kev for my new Goth outlook on life, much as I'd like to.

I know someone who has to Hoover before *anyone* comes into the house – even if someone else has only been (and he has Hoovered) twenty minutes before. If that isn't strange enough, he has to do his carpets like his lawn: down, turn, up, turn, down, leaving perfect stripes. I imagine by now, like football club groundsmen, he has graduated to creating beautiful criss-cross patterns or concentric circles.

I need a victory over Preston today to exorcise all these irrelevant FA Cup shenanigans. I'm starting to obsess about Kevin Keegan, which can't be healthy for anyone.

I love the ebb and flow of a town on match day. In Stoke, the early drinkers start arriving at about noon, and they wash around the pubs, spilling from this one to that. By one o'clock, the town's flooded with fans, but by two, there's a definite drift towards the stadium, a steady current of people walking out of town or catching the laid-on buses. Shortly after two-thirty, the swell has almost gone, leaving little pools of fans standing outside the pubs, smoking, more concerned with getting in another pint than getting to the game on time – or at all. I've often been tempted to stay in town to see it empty and then refill as the tide comes in again after the match, but I never have and I don't today.

We're pretty good. Solid and professional, we win 3-1 and that night I realise the therapy's worked – I lie in bed, forcing myself to think about Kevin Keegan (not something I would recommend unless, as in this case, it's for medical purposes) and for the first time in a while I don't want to tan his Messiah arse with a cricket bat.

Maybe when Peter Coates gets home he wears a squirty flower in his lapel, keeps the whole family in stitches with a huge repertoire of gags and a whoopee cushion before dragging everyone round the piano to belt out Chas & Dave songs, but somehow I doubt it. Our chairman is an undemonstrative sort of man, almost dour, at least in public.

God alone knows why, closer to seventy than sixty, he would want to come back and run this club. To head for the trenches again, battle-weary and shell-shocked from a first tour of duty which ended in violence, threats to him and his family and a legacy of dislike for him and mistrust of him from nearly every Stoke City fan.

He controlled the club during one of its least successful and most turbulent periods since we were formed in 1863, although arguably the carpet had been pulled out from under him long before he picked up the poisoned chalice. The fortunes of Stoke-on-Trent's dominant team have pretty much mirrored the fortunes of its dominant industry since the mid-1970s. The realisation that you could make a plate almost for free in China or Indonesia, currency fluctuations and a move away from formal dining did for the pottery industry, as the roof blowing off the Butler Street Stand of the Victoria Ground did for Stoke City.

In the four years running up to the storm in January 1976 that peeled off the roof, we had lifted the League Cup at Wembley Stadium, played in the European Cup, had a couple of top-five finishes and reached the semi-final of the FA Cup twice. And bear in mind this was a time when the FA Cup was a prize akin to the Holy Grail, not the annoying distraction it has become for big clubs today; a competition graced by near-reserve teams where any old tin-pot outfit has a half-decent chance of making it to the final. Okay, I admit it, any old tin-pot outfit except Stoke who still, I believe, have one of the very worst cup records in history. Even if it's not *the* very worst record for league teams, it certainly feels like it, and suffice to say, when some rag-tag bunch of non-league cloggers from Nether Scrote or Lower Itching draw us out of the bag (or whatever it is they use these days; I think they may have gone all razzmatazz and upgraded to classy clear plastic) they stick a tenner on themselves and put the champagne on ice.

As the dust settled on the wooden seats of the Butler Street Stand, it transpired there were insurance 'issues', in the same way that there were health issues after the Chernobyl disaster. Roughly translated, it meant we had no insurance, and the only way of avoiding going bust within months was to sell a host of players, among them some of the greatest ever to pull on a Stoke shirt – Alan Hudson, our arrogant, visionary, gifted midfielder went to Arsenal, while striker Jimmy Greenhoff was transferred to Manchester United. Inevitably, we were relegated that season.

Incidentally, Hudson was co-author of a book called *The Working Man's Ballet* and I can't think of a better phrase to encapsulate the beauty of football, especially the sort of football Hudson himself played, seemingly oblivious to anything except the need to demonstrate his own superiority. The phrase, incidentally, was coined by Tony Waddington, Stoke's greatest manager. It's no coincidence the organisers of the Italia 90 World Cup opted for Pavarotti singing *Nessun Dorma* as their theme tune. The undulating, swelling drama of the piece is the perfect musical reflection of a great game or a fantastic goal.

Admittedly, opera becomes a tad less dramatic when you realise what's being said. Every so often my mum and dad would try to instill a bit of cultural appreciation in me and sit me down in front of some BBC2 production. I quite enjoyed some of the music, but the effect was ruined by the mundane, stilted and repetitive text of the subtitles.

Scorchio: My heart soars like the eagle when I see you!

Chlamydia: Desist, you knave.

Scorchio: But my heart soars!

Chlamydia: Desist, I say, I must go shopping.

Scorchio: My heart soars!

Chlamydia: I need some courgettes.

Scorchio: It soars!

Chlamydia: And some bread.

Scorchio: Soars!

Chlamydia: And some radishes.

Scorchio: Soars!

Chlamydia: Radishes!

Scorchio: Soars!

Chlamydia: Radishes!

And so on.

The beautiful has certainly been a bit thin on the ground this season, but there's been no shortage of the dramatic. But Stoke's fortunes since those January gales have been more tragedy than anything else, although I suppose we should be thankful we were still at the Victoria Ground, nestled on the valley floor rather than at our new site on top of Hurricane Hill.

If the wind was strong enough to blow the roof off part of the Vic, it would have lifted the Britannia Stadium clean off its foundations and deposited it in front of a slightly alarmed farmer half way to Derby. There was a wonderful, last-gasp victory at Notts County to take us back to the First Division in 1979, but that came to an end in 1985 when we were despatched back to the Second Division with our tail between our legs and, at the time, the fewest points ever collected by a team in the top flight of English football.

We won seventeen points from a possible hundred and twenty-six, we won three out of forty-two league games and we scored twenty-four goals, of which only six were at away games. We let in ninety-one goals and twice lost ten games on the run. When we played Arsenal at home at the end of March, just over seven thousand fans turned up. And boldly ignoring the traditionally-favoured option of having relegation confirmed in the dying seconds of injury time of the last game of the season as someone scores hundreds of miles away, our fate was sealed in April, with seven games to go. Happy days.

Over the same period, the pottery industry was heading in a similar direction. In 1970 it employed fifty thousand people – a third of the entire workforce. A *third*. In 1980 it was thirty thousand, and by 1996 it was probably a little over twenty thousand as cheap imports took their toll and mechanisation and mergers led to decreasing demand for the skilled workers of the past. In the five years between 2001 and 2006, more than five thousand jobs were lost and at least fifty ceramic companies disappeared.

The trend is for the big, household name, global brand companies to source products from the Far East or South America or Eastern Europe, or to set up dedicated factories over there. And why wouldn't they? If it's a choice between cutting jobs in Stoke-on-Trent and closing altogether, it's a pretty simple equation. Some of the lower-volume, higher-value ware is still made here, partly, in some cases, so that they have something for the coachloads of Americans and Japanese to see before they're funnelled into the factory shop and relieved of as much cash as possible.

Sometimes I suspect each of the large firms only employs about eight people – one to turn the lights on and sit behind reception to greet the tourists and seven to sit there painting plates while the visitors file past, herded by the guide towards the double doors and retail heaven. As soon as they're gone, I imagine the seven slumping back and playing cards, reading or knitting until a red light flashes above the door, signalling the arrival of another coachload of dollars. In a few years I imagine we'll be known as the Call Centres, rather than the Potteries, or the Distribution Centres.

I'm exaggerating, of course, and there are still probably more than two hundred ceramic companies in North Staffordshire – some of them many years old, employing hundreds of people locally and doing quite nicely, thank you, while others are smaller, newer, and operating in niche markets, charging a premium for cutting edge design or exceptional quality. In terms of employment, though, the pottery industry will undoubtedly shrink further, and the threat of redundancy is a way of life for thousands of workers and their families here.

In a roundabout way, I think what I'm saying is we – both Stoke-on-Trent and Stoke City – could do with a bit of a break. We're used to being rubbish at football, losing our jobs, surviving on low wages and putting up with high crime levels and poor health, but a joke's a joke and we could just do with a bit of a rest. A bit of jam with our bread – surely that's not too much to ask for.

When Peter Coates took control of the club for the first

time, just after we were relegated in 1985, we thought he was the all natural, made to Granny Griffiths' secret recipe, one hundred per cent fruit preserve we'd been waiting for. But it wasn't to be. Barring a couple of minor cups and a play-off victory, underachievement was the order of the day and Coates was accused of cashing in on key players just as it looked like we could get back into the top flight. Boycotts, protests and intimidation took their toll, and he sold out to an Icelandic consortium in 1999, although he kept a seat on the board.

Tony Pulis was brought in by the new owners on Coates's recommendation in November 2002. In a farce typical of the club at the time, Gudjon Thordarson, the manager initially brought in by the Icelanders, had been sacked immediately after winning promotion to the Championship, replacement Steve Cotterill blew any chance of receiving the much-coveted Stoke City long service carriage clock by bailing out of his contract after thirteen games over five months to take up a better offer as assistant manager of Sunderland, and the club organised a press conference to unveil George Burley as the manager – an appointment which was almost universally welcomed by Stoke fans.

Unfortunately, George never turned up to the press conference and the longer the cameramen and journalists twiddled their thumbs, the more obvious it became he hadn't just taken the wrong junction off the M6.

So Pulis wasn't the board's first choice and he certainly wasn't the fans' first choice either. During his first game at Walsall, a sizeable section of the Stoke following gave him a rendition of the classic 'You Don't Know What You're Doing', a chant usually reserved for managers who have been at a club considerably longer than ninety minutes and incompetent referees and linesmen (by which, of course, I mean referees and referee's assistants who give decisions which annoy us, rather than decisions which are necessarily incorrect).

He didn't win any of his first ten league games in charge and by then many fans' poor opinion of him was set in stone.

Against the odds, he kept us up that season, and the next season, 2003/2004, wasn't too bad either. But the following season was dire. Not in terms of where we ended up – we finished twelfth; our defence was far too good for us to go down – but because of the numbing monotony of many of the games we had to sit through.

Alan Durban, the manager who guided us to that promotion to the old First Division in 1979, once said: 'If you want entertainment, go and watch a bunch of clowns,' and at the moment I'd take success over entertainment like a shot. But 2004/2005 was taking the piss and it became known as the binary season because the results of our games seemed to be just a series of zeros and ones.

The relationship between the manager and the Icelandic owners was falling apart and, with the alarming sense of timing for which the board had become known, Pulis was sacked a few weeks after he had been given a new contract. Coates had been making noises in the background about being willing to take over the reins again, but the Icelanders held out and appointed eccentric Dutchman Johan Boskamp as manager. When that went tits-up, the Icelanders realised they would be better off financially if they sat at home in Reykjavik burning fistfuls of kronur instead of running a mediocre club in one of England's poorest cities, and Peter Coates took back control in the summer of 2006. He immediately reappointed Tony Pulis. So here they were again – an unpopular manager foisted on mutinous fans by an even more unpopular chairman. Balls the size of Wales, the pair of them.

There were a few chants of 'Pulis out' at the start of last season, and someone was trying to co-ordinate a protest involving 10,000 fans holding up red cards, although the idea was eventually abandoned after a couple of loan signings poured oil on troubled waters. Since then, in spite of relatively healthy league positions, most fans have tolerated both chairman and manager rather than warmed to them, unprepared to give up grudges and unwilling to trust that things will be different this time.

I include myself in that category, even though we're fourth in the table, a point off an automatic promotion place and unbeaten in twelve games. We'd drawn the four league games before the victory over Preston, and the fear that we're going to slide down the table is never far away. If we do, and the season runs up a dead end again, the honeymoon period for Coates and Pulis will be well and truly over, their fates sealed and their shot at redemption – if that's what it is – gone forever.

For a lot of that post-1985 period my own circumstances mirrored those of the club – a skint underachiever surviving from one week to the next. Whether I was cleaning toilets in Greece, cleaning cars in Stoke-on-Trent or failing to flog a whole variety of products due to my almost complete inability to sell, my financial situation started to make Stoke City look positively flush. I was living with Ash in a terrace just down from Hanley bus station, and turning the house upside down for loose change was a weekly occurrence. Not for luxuries like food, but for one of the small packs of rolling tobacco from the twenty-four-hour garage a hundred yards down the road.

I can think of no better illustration of the horrific power of addiction than Ash and me making roll-ups out of tea leaves when we could only find seven pence down the back of the sofa. Most of the leaves ended up in your mouth, sticking uncomfortably to the back of your throat and the inside of your cheeks, while the rest either didn't catch or combusted to dust in a millisecond. Thinking about it, maybe if they'd had resealable tabs in those days it would have been different. Maybe the fresh, moist leaves would have caught and smouldered beautifully, giving long, satisfying minutes of smoking pleasure from a single pinch.

Ash's psychotic cats refused to downsize with us. As our fortunes plummeted, we tried to wean them on to food which cost about three pence a can and consisted of eighty-five per cent wood chippings, fourteen per cent abattoir scrapings and one per cent recycled plastic cups, but they weren't fooled, the furry little fuckers, and refused to eat. After a stand-off of a few days we cracked (or, more accurately, Ash cracked; I would happily have taken them to the cats' home) and we had to sit there watching them eat their top-of-the-range foie gras and truffle oil-infused chunks coated with delicious platinum dust jelly while we ate Tesco Value sausages in Tesco Value sliced white.

I suggested we eat the cats, which would solve all our problems, but Ash seemed reluctant for some reason. My next idea, to try smoking the half-inch layer of fur they left over every room in the house, fell on deaf ears as well. At the time, it seemed a reasonable compromise to harvest a useful and sustainable crop from them, but I accept I may have been drinking and malnutrition might have clouded my judgement.

But my fortunes changed (as did Ash's, although those bloody cats are still snuffling round his house, wearing tiaras and emitting beluga caviar-scented farts every eight seconds) and, in spite of being pretty much unemployable and unmarriable, I ended up with a house I can just about afford and a beautiful wife and boy who – on a good day – quite like me.

There are signs the city's fortunes are also about to take a turn for the better. Billions of pounds are being bussed into the area to tackle deprivation and the problems associated with it, and a new wave of creative businesses and young entrepreneurs could help pull the Potteries back into the light.

Now we need the club to come along for the ride and to help us get there. To get us promoted and put us on the map, so that kids in Thailand, China, Africa and Australia see us on the TV and ask each other 'Where the hell's Stoke?' before lying on the floor, atlas open, finger exploring the page before coming to rest under Stoke-on-Trent, the insignificant dot between Manchester and Birmingham that has the gravitational pull of a planet for so many of us.

We need to keep this unbeaten run going and we need to turn the draws into wins to rebuild the season's momentum and give us all something to believe in.

The following week we lose away at Charlton. They're now level with us on points.

To: Ford Motor Company

Much as I'd like to, as an avid football fan I find it impossible to miss the adverts you have on before, during and after the live games you sponsor on satellite telly. One that is repeated ad nauseam, to the point of me wanting to sandpaper my own eyeballs in a no doubt futile attempt to take away the pain of having to sit through it again, involves hundreds of people tying balloons to their vehicles and, with sadness in their eyes, watching them float off over the cityscape. The cars float off, I mean, not the people's eyes. I'm assuming it would be physically impossible to watch your own eyes float away, although I'm no doctor.

I may be wrong (a rare but not completely unknown occurrence) but I think the idea is that these poor unfortunates have just seen the new Ford Bland, or whatever it is, slinking down the mean streets of the city, and, knowing their own motors will never measure up, they get busy with the balloons.

Quite apart from the obvious safety issues here – when the balloons start popping, all those Blands and their proud owners are going to be pulverised as it starts raining inferior makes of car – I have serious reservations about the financial sense of getting rid of your shameful jalopy in this manner. Surely if a glimpse of a Bland (model featured the Bland Turbo Fallus, from £860,000) changes people's perceptions of personal transport forever, they will want to buy one quick snap. What do they now have to trade in? Nothing, that's what, unless you count one of those balloon pump things.

I know those underpaid advertising types are just trying to get a message across, but do me a favour and take it off. My eyeballs are bleeding and I come from Stoke-on-Trent: life's hard enough without having to sit through this garbage sixty times a match.

Much appreciated.

David Johnson

CHAPTER 15

It takes a bloody lifetime to get to the Cardiff game because Andy's torn the ligaments in his ankle and he can hardly walk. He was working up in Scotland, had a couple of drinks at night and asked the taxi driver to drop him by the back entrance to the hotel so he could just hop over that three-foot wall. Unfortunately, on the other side of the three-foot wall there was a twelve-foot drop, hence today's slow progress as we finally make it up Cardiac Hill, Andy dragging his foot behind him.

As the teams warm up, Andy tells us his new girlfriend was called out three times last night. His voice full of admiration, Ash asks if she's a prostitute. He doesn't sound convinced when he's told Fiona is a physiotherapist (a happy coincidence given the current state of Andy's ankle) and he keeps asking for her number and whether she does call-outs.

I'm fed up with trying to predict what's going to happen this season, although I know I'll keep doing it. One week we're fantastic, the next we're dire. We're desperate for a win against Cardiff, another team who could be towards the top of the table in May, and the boys duly come out and give us a 2-1 victory. Sidibe misses two easy chances to open his account twenty-one games into the season – *twenty-one!* – but Griffin, Lawrence and Fuller are excellent. We're still fourth, but with tough games coming up, this is a great result against a good team. And doubts about Peter Coates's intentions during the last transfer window, or his willingness to put his hand in his pocket when it really matters, have disappeared. In the twenty-four hours before the January trading deadline passed in the run-up to the Cardiff game, we sold John

Eustace to our promotion rivals Watford for £250,000 – the second captain we have sold this season.

But we buy Sheffield Wednesday midfielder Glenn Whelan for £500,000 and we sign Blackburn striker Paul Gallagher on a loan deal. Earlier in the month, Pulis and Coates agreed permanent deals for Ryan Shawcross, Leon Cort, Andy Griffin and Danny Pugh – all of whom look like they would run over broken glass for the team and seem to be really good players individually. There's still a debate going on between fans about whether Pulis is using the talent and commitment at his disposal effectively, but since the turn of the year, Peter Coates has signed cheques to the tune of around £3.5m. If it's redemption he's after, it's not coming cheap.

We all return, time and again, to the places we feel most comfortable or where we have experienced deep emotions. For me it's the Victoria Ground, the Britannia Stadium and Cornwall. For Alison it's the Lake District and the Clinique counter at Boots.

Both Cornwall and Stoke City have been an important part of my life for longer than I can remember. A lot of my mum's side of the family were from around Paul, Mousehole, Newlyn and Penzance and we went down there at least twice a year. Scrabble through the drawers at my mum and dad's house or our house or my sister's and you'll find wallet after wallet of photos of us all, at all stages of our lives, on some beach or clifftop, or looking slightly bored outside some West Country stately home.

We used to stay in an ancient caravan in my nan's garden. It still had gas lights inside, although my grandad had since wired it up to the mains, and a stable door that didn't really fit. Every year, a little bit more of the caravan would have fallen off or caved in and there would be fresh patches of filler painted over to blend as well as possible. All the wooden panels had bowed in and the decades of increasingly desperate repairs gave the whole thing a lumpy look as if it had been made out of mashed potato and left to dry. It was paradise.

Tales about things we did and places we went when I was one, two or three years old have become as easy to picture as events I can genuinely remember, and these inherited memories merge with the real thing from about the age of four onwards.

Digging out sand boats on Porthgwarra, almost stepping on a snake on the cliff top above Porthcurno, making up stories in the caravan for my sister when we should have been going to sleep and the strange way my mum and dad's voices seemed to come from miles away, from somewhere out to sea, when they came to bed talking softly and I was half asleep and half awake.

Me and my sister racing up the lane, one on the scooter and the other running, to the Norths' farm and shouting to Kim the Alsatian to come for his breakfast of my grandad's bacon scraps and us racing back down the lane and him racing across the field between my nan's house and the farm.

Later, I remember reading western after western from my grandad's bespittled, yellowing stockpile, and later still guiltily combing the damp-smelling pile of ten-year-old *Cosmopolitan* and *She* magazines for pictures of impossibly exotic women in bikinis and lingerie while my hormones fizzed and exploded and my heart thumped the inside of my ribcage. Getting seasick on the boat to the Isles of Scilly and even sicker on a fishing trip in a tiny orange boat with a butcher called Kneebone.

Memories of getting drunk with my mates, usually failing to pull girls at Demelza's in Penzance, play-fighting under my nan's window at three in the morning and Nige holding my arm while Mark jabbed away with a penknife and smudged the ink from a ballpoint to tattoo what looked like a sparrow, although it was meant to be a swallow. Of snogs on street corners, please-God-let-her-sleep-with-me weekends with new girlfriends, a reconciliation weekend with a girlfriend who had slept with her ex-boyfriend, an unforgettable night in the Ship Inn on Mousehole harbour, the whole place lit with candles because the worst January storm in years had taken the power out, wonderful days with my wife-to-be and now family holidays with our son.

Almost without being aware of it I will try to pass on my love of this place to my son as surely as I will try to turn him into a Stoke fan.

It's not really the memories of specific events, though, that bind me to Cornwall; it's the way the whole place made – and still makes – me feel. The sense that I belong, that I'm welcome, that my life can be played to slightly different rules and the almost immediate slump of relaxation I feel as soon as I pass the 'Welcome to Cornwall' sign.

It's the hours on end I would spend lying on the bed in the caravan, watching perfect white clouds slide across the blue rectangle of sky defined by the open top of the stable doorway, the sound of the rain on the caravan roof and the hours, days, weeks and months of my life I must have spent exploring the rockpools, cliffs and coves between Mousehole and Lamorna.

I know a lot of it's seen through rose-tinted spectacles, and things certainly changed over the years. Norths' field sprouted a crop of bungalows ages ago, and the new house to the front a couple of years later meant you had to stand on tiptoes, or climb into the tree in the corner, to see the long strip of sea – powder blue, sapphire, jade, turquoise or grey depending on the weather – half a mile away down the hillside.

It's the same with Stoke. When I started this book I imagined reminiscing about famous victories in great detail and writing about the humiliation of losing 8-0 to Liverpool in 2000 and 7-0 to Birmingham in 1997. The truth is, I can remember the occasional fantastic win or shaming loss over the years, the triumphs and disasters which punctuate every football fan's life, but mainly it's the senses that I keep coming back to. The sound of the Boothen End at the Victoria Ground, the smell of the toilets, the splash of urine underfoot, and the rush of excitement every time Mark Chamberlain got the ball.

I can remember some things in great detail, seemingly randomly, although I'm sure there's some deep psychological reason for them being etched indelibly on my memory like a crap tattoo of a sparrow. Trying to catch the bus back from Stoke with my sister on New Year's Day, somehow not realising the buses wouldn't run on a bank holiday.

We trudged back to the phone box near the ground and as the snow came down in those big, slow flakes that let you know they mean business, a battered Austin Princess pulled up and Georgie Berry, still this club's best-loved cult hero, gave us a lift back home. I can't remember if it was before or after this, but my sister and I met Georgie again when we were kids and we asked him to autograph a picture of him in action in the programme. The only photo we could find was of him looking like he was completely missing the ball, although his afro was as impressive as ever, which counts for a lot in a cult hero.

'It's no wonder I keep missing the ball, is it?' he asked, holding up a pair of glasses that looked like they were double-glazed. 'I can't see a bloody thing without these.'

Now I'm forcing myself to pin down memories from my football-watching career, I can't believe how many Georgie Berry stories there are, and I suppose that's why he's still loved by Stoke fans. He acted the buffoon so much it's easy to forget he played at the highest level in England, won the League Cup with Wolves and was capped five times for Wales. The last time I saw him he had been substituted and within minutes he was on the Boothen End, singing his heart out for the lads. Again, I couldn't say which game it was, although I've got a feeling it was the last time he played for us.

I remember me and my sister legging it when a bit of trouble broke out after a game and a Forest fan who looked like a trainspotter drew a hammer from his anorak and started screaming: 'Come on, then, who wants it?' and running at everyone trying to brain them with Stanley's finest. I think this has stayed with me because we were with a couple of kids our age who we didn't really know but who were the children of family friends.

They were Liverpool fans and the fact that a bloke who looked like a serial killer was running around with a hammer didn't seem to worry them; in fact they seemed to think it was pretty funny. I remember thinking we had let ourselves, our club and our city down by turning tail rather than facing death by DIY. Even then I took an unhealthy, secret pride in the notorious reputation of some of our fans. I despise football violence, but I still find it difficult not to stick out my chest a bit when someone asks me who I support, I tell them Stoke and they widen their eyes, puff out their cheeks and say: 'Not one of *those* Stoke fans, I hope.'

'No, no,' I laugh, reassuringly, but with what I hope is enough of an air of evasiveness and mystery to leave them with the impression I may actually be a veteran of decades of fights, now promoted to General, directing trouble from the safety of a mobile, confident no-one would suspect this balding bloke with man-boobs of being one of the country's most wanted hooligans.

But generally, like I say, it's the feeling of these places, the comforting routine of going to the game or heading south at holiday time, the framework of the familiar which keeps you standing firm in the face of the relentless crap that life throws at you.

There's a photograph I see every few years, although I

can't seem to put my hands on it now, and it shows us on the beach at Porthgwarra in front of the huge boulder, more than ten feet high, where we used to sit. My grandad is sitting in a deckchair, trousers rolled up and his hands clasped on the bend of his walking stick, my sister's there and I'm there, no doubt called back from the water for the photo, and my mum's there too.

I think my nan's on it, although I couldn't swear to it, and I guess my dad was behind the camera. There we all are, three generations frozen in a fading gloss print, and my great-grandparents and great-great-grandparents must have stood in exactly the same spot. You can feel that connection with the past and it's the same with Stoke.

I suppose at times it was a chore for my dad, an Everton fan, to take us to the match every other week, and I know my parents grew to despise the long haul down the motorway to Cornwall, forced to drive for half a day in holiday traffic by the duty to see your family.

Just thinking about that photograph, I can fool myself into smelling the salt on the granite and feeling the cold ridges of a limpet on the boulder behind me, and I can remember the wince-inducing brightness of the tiny, whitewashed shop at the top of the causeway where we'd buy Sherbet Fountains.

One of the last times I saw my nan she was standing in the window of her room in the old folks' home on the main road, watching the cars.

'I just don't understand it,' she said. 'All those people driving this way, all these others driving that way. If they all just swapped places then no-one would have to drive anywhere.'

It's possible she was some sort of green guru, acutely aware of the implications of increasing road traffic ten years ahead of her time, but she'd pretty much lost her marbles at this point, so I wouldn't bank on it. Either way, it was shortly after this I stopped going to Cornwall for a few years, probably because I felt guilty about avoiding going to see my nan as she slipped further into dementia.

There were a few years when I didn't go to the game much, either, when I was working away cleaning toilets in Greece, washing dishes in Austria or failing to find a job I really wanted to do in other parts of this country. But I went back to Cornwall, just as I knew I would, and, just as I knew I would, I came back to Stoke-on-Trent and Stoke City.

Alison's muttering something about there being some erratic dishwasher loading going on, but the game away at Wolves is too exciting and I find it impossible to care whether my top-tray performance has hit the bare minimum ninety per cent space utilisation target.

'It's not erratic,' I tell her, waving my hand at her to be quiet, 'it's innovative.'

'Innovative my–' but at that moment, four minutes in, Rory Delap nods us in front, and the sound of more than two thousand Stoke fans bursting into uncontrolled celebration sends me hopping round the kitchen, grinning from ear to ear and waving the dirty chopping board in the air – an unfortunate manoeuvre which flicks raw chicken in all directions.

It's a great game, one of those matches that's almost impossible to listen to because of that distilled terror you get listening to radio commentary, the heightened dread every time the other team attacks, unseen, in a strange stadium miles away. I'm still considering whether to tell Alison about the piece of poultry skin in her hair when Wolves equalise just before half-time. Just after half-time they go in front, but the awful nausea of disappointment only lasts two minutes before Lawrence scores a fantastic equaliser. The atmosphere is manic, and I wish I was there. It goes off the scale when big Mama, still unable to score, heads against the bar and Cort prods in the rebound to put us 3-2 up.

The final twenty minutes are end to end and filled with

chances – Wolves will end up having eighteen goal attempts while we will have thirteen – and I'm stalking from room to room, my nerves singing. Then, in the last minute, just when I think I can't take any more, Fuller breaks away from our besieged goal, runs more than half the length of the pitch, holds off two defenders and buries the ball across the keeper and into the net.

With a third of the campaign to go our team, reviled for its negative tactics, has already scored sixteen goals more than during the entire binary season of 2005/2006, and I'm daring to dream again.

CHAPTER 16

I'm finding it difficult to get on with the book; there are just too many distractions.

Tonight, Alison comes in and tells me she needs my input to choosing a new kitchen, that she doesn't want to be the one making all the decisions and that I need to take some responsibility.

If she was after a go-getting decision-maker who thrives on responsibility, I suggest, perhaps she should have avoided marrying someone who knew her for fifteen years before popping the question. Anyway, I tell her, I haven't got time to take any responsibility because, in case she'd forgotten or thought that all these late nights at the computer were some sort of attempt at breaking the world record for the consumption of internet porn, I'm writing a bestseller about Stoke getting promoted to the Premier League.

She asks me about the two decades she knew me when I wasn't writing a book and still refused to take responsibility for anything, but that's just a cheap shot and I'm not afraid to say so. In any case, I go on, if I *don't* write a bestseller about Stoke being promoted to the Premier League, we won't be able to *afford* a new kitchen.

'Do you think Anne Hathaway used to keep bothering Shakespeare about what colour curtains they should have when he was busy producing the greatest literary works in the history of the written word?

'Do you think he'd be sitting there at the dining room table, just like I am, candle burning, scratching his head muttering: "Shall I compare thee to a ... to a ... oh, bugger ... to a ... chilly morning ... no ... April shower ... no, no ...

hang on, hang on, of course, I've got it!" and then in blunders Hathaway looking all flustered, saying: "Bill, the wattle and daub man's here and he wants to know if we want pox scab red or open sewer brown."

'I don't bloody think so, do you?'

She tells me to get over myself and look at these brochures right bloody now.

An hour later, I'm back at the dining room table. If you're interested, I quite fancy the Kelmscott Oak from MFI.

The home game against Southampton is on Tuesday night. The day is a stereotypical, straight-from-childhood winter's day: crisp frost, blinding white sun and a sky which is the shade of blue you only usually see when you're in a plane above the clouds.

The weather probably contributes to the strange feeling I've been getting lately. I can't quite pin it down, but it's not unpleasant and it's vaguely familiar, as if I've experienced it before, but a long time ago. Can it really be? It is, you know. It's that mild but constant adrenalin trickle you get before matches when your team's doing well and looking like the real deal, fuelled by an uplifting yet relaxing cocktail of excitement, optimism, hope and confidence.

I'm genuinely starting to believe this team won't buckle and capitulate like so many others I've seen over the years, that we have the right blend of skills and temperaments to deal with the pressure and that they are focused on winning promotion with a clarity that matches the brilliant blue of the morning.

Just over 19,000 people come to the game, and I can tell I'm not the only one who has been possessed by this unfamiliar positive streak. From the first whistle, we completely dominate the game and Southampton look every inch a club floating about near the relegation zone – weak and hopeless at the back, and when they start arguing with each other you just know we've got them.

The first goes in after a demented scramble in the six-yard box on twenty-seven minutes, after one of their defenders opts for sticking the ball in his own net rather than the more traditional approach of making a clearance. Less than ten minutes later, Ryan Shawcross heads in his eighth goal of the season, and a minute before half-time, after six long, barren months, our allergic-to-scoring striker Mama Sidibe gets his first of the season. Even as we're celebrating this novel feat of winning a game before the second half has even started, none of us can quite believe what's happened.

'Was it Mama?' we ask each other, eyes wide. 'It was Mama, wasn't it? I'm sure it was.'

I can't recall a regular striker ever going two-thirds of the season without scoring in the league, not just at Stoke but at any club, and it certainly wouldn't have happened without vitriolic opposition from the stands and heated questions being asked about the manager's suitability for continued employment. There's a huge amount of goodwill for Mama, not really because just a few weeks ago he was almost hacked to death, but because his commitment and effort are totally unquestionable. I don't know if it's the same at other clubs, but Stoke fans can forgive pretty much anything as long as they believe you sweat blood for the red and white stripes, although admittedly being a striker and not scoring until the end of the season is in sight has pushed us pretty close to breaking point.

So when we all finally come to terms with what our eyes have seen a few moments before, and we accept that Mama has indeed scored, the celebrations are loud, long and warm. I'm amazed the Southampton players don't all just trudge from the field and get back on the bus to the south coast, too dejected to shower or change. When Mama Sidibe scores against you, you know it's time to look yourself in the eye, hand in your notice and retrain as an accounting technician or driving instructor – your footballing days are done.

So it's 3-0 at half-time, Southampton aren't even in the game and it looks like we may finally have a group of players which is capable of putting poor teams to the sword, breaking their spirit with our physical strength and mental toughness.

Yeah, right. Southampton come out in the second half like Brazil on crack. After eleven seconds – that's right, eleven seconds – Stern John flicks the ball over Shawcross and buries an unstoppable volley from outside the area. Eight minutes later he scores again and we go to pieces in spectacular fashion. John has chance after chance as our defenders fall over each other in panic, Simmo races around his six-yard box like a crazed dog in a pen, and everyone gets in everyone else's way because there are so many people crammed into one third of the pitch. The confidence of players and fans is shot, and although Simmo makes a great save (from John yet again; he must have had a gargantuan hit on the pipe at half-time) we know it's only a matter of time.

With about twenty minutes to go, a Southampton player has a shot from outside the box. Simmo's got it covered, but it takes a huge deflection, and it spins and curls towards the opposite corner of the goal. I'm right in line with it, and it's going in, no doubt about it. It feels like the ball takes about four days to reach the goal, but every player on the pitch and it seems every fan in the stadium is rooted to the spot, motionless, watching its sedate approach to the line until, when all hope seems to have gone, the spin exhausts itself, the trajectory straightens and the ball skims past the post to safety.

Finally, in the last fifteen minutes, the Southampton players seem to sense they've got nothing left to chuck at us (or maybe the hard drugs are wearing off), we stop treating them as if they're eleven Maradonas armed with sawn-off shotguns and we squeak a win. But this habit of pressing the panic button and seemingly doing everything we can to throw away victories is playing havoc with my nerves, and I'm not sure how much more I can take.

Here are the three worst people I've sat next to:

1. The bloke on the train to Cornwall one year. At first glance he didn't look overly insane, and I congratulated myself on bagging one of the last seats – standing all the way to Penzance didn't really hold much appeal. He would write in his notepad, sit up and stare out of the window for a second, or scratch his chin as if he was giving his words great thought, before hunching over the pad again. When he shifted his weight slightly a few minutes later I could see what he was writing: 'Jesus won over sin Jesus won over sin Jesus won over sin Jesus won over sin Jesus won over sin.' The full stop's mine, by the way; this guy had no need for such worldly punctuation and he carried on like this, filling page after page after page.

Now Jesus may well have won over sin, I don't feel sufficiently theologically qualified to get into that argument, but I do believe I have enough knowledge of basic psychiatry to say in all confidence that writing 'Jesus won over sin' 7,384 times – especially with your tongue sticking out of the corner of your mouth – is not normal behaviour. It is, in fact, the action of someone who not only has one of those fish symbols on the back of his car, but also has one of those fish symbols tattooed across the breadth of his back and who walks around with barbed wire in his underpants as a constant reminder of our Lord's suffering and to stifle any impure thoughts with a sharp jab to the scrotum.

He never tried to engage me in wild, scary religious conversation (I'd already decided to go for the classic deaf mute act if he did), but the fear that he would made for a distinctly uncomfortable four or five hours before he got off at Bristol Temple Meads, presumably to go on some sort of mass killing spree before turning the gun on himself.

2. The girl in the call centre where I used to work who had a reputation for being especially free with her affections. Almost every morning she would come in, hungover to hell, and tell us about the previous night's victim. Or victims. Once she was off work for three days because her throat and mouth had swollen up to alarming proportions after a particularly unhygienic amorous encounter round the back of some nightclub. Now I can't exactly take the moral high ground here, and under certain circumstances I'd probably enjoy lapping up (oh, please!) all the salacious details, but this woman was no Catherine Zeta-Jones and any pleasurable titillation was destroyed by the stench of layer upon layer of old sweat (usually not just her own), stale vodka, and, let's not beat around the bush, bodily fluids. Summer was the worst. Her sap was on the rise, warmer nights meant opportunities for multiple al fresco liaisons were much more frequent and the next day, as the sun beat down on us, polarised through the glass of the tall windows, the fetid stink rising from her was truly retch-inducing.

3. The two cocks who sit a couple of seats away from us at the Scunthorpe game.

Southampton was on the Tuesday, and we play Scunthorpe on the Friday night, so if we win we go top, at least until everyone else plays on the Saturday. Southampton were pretty near the bottom, but Scunthorpe actually *are* bottom, and that treacherous optimism starts to trickle back into my veins, conning me into hope and then certainty. By the time

I leave work on Friday, I know we will be top of the league within five hours.

Who you have sitting round you at a football match, as in so many other arenas of life, can make or destroy your day.

Around us it is mainly groups of friends or families who've been sitting in the same seats season after season. You can tell some are related, but you never know for certain because conversations in the stands rarely become personal, even though one of the most powerful attractions of supporting a team – that sense of belonging and attachment to thousands of other people – comes straight from the core of your psyche. Maybe that's a big part of the attraction: an instant sense of community without the hassle of any great emotional investment, at least with each other. Even within our own groups, we don't really talk about anything of depth. In our case we tend to talk about football or breasts. That's not a macho thing, even though we're all men in our clique; it's just that you instinctively avoid talking about anything of great import at a game. Maybe it's an escape thing.

Maybe part of the irresistible pull to football stadia is because we all know, no matter what country we come from, that for a couple of hours we can leave work worries, family problems, class differences and financial woes at the turnstile. In our case, though, I'm pretty sure we talk about football and breasts just because football and breasts interest us more than just about anything else in the world.

The people you sit next to at the game are usually a strange mix you will never see together anywhere else except maybe at your wedding. You just seem to accumulate each other as the years go by, and by your late twenties that's pretty much it, membership is set for life and the group dynamic is cast in stone. I even know cases where men who have been through nasty, cruel divorces have carried on going to the game with their ex-wives' fathers or brothers.

I sit with Andy (my brother-in-law), Ash (one of my best

mates from school), Robbo (who became a mate when we worked at the same place more than ten years ago) and Alison's cousin Dave. I see Robbo every other week from mid-August to the beginning of May, and then nothing until, on the morning of the new season, a text will pop up: 'Going for beer before?'

We all renew our season tickets in exactly the same seats every year, even if a reshuffle might be advisable. I sit between Robbo and cousin Dave, who are both footie anoraks, and they talk statistics across me all game, occasionally forgetting I won't have a clue what they're talking about and trying to include me in their conversations.

'Who's the ref, cousin Dave? It looks like Bob Throckett.'

'No, it's Derek Thistleblower from Keighley, the one who sent off Andy Griffin in the reserve game against Bury in 1997. September, it was.'

'Oh, bloody hell, yeah, and remember that penalty he never gave when we played Bradford in ninety-three in the pre-season friendly?'

'I know, we've got no chance if he's reffing. Isn't that Peter van de Piper on their bench? Used to play for Barnet, Wolves, Gretna, Barnsley, Oldham, Barnsley again and then Plymouth.'

'No, you're completely wrong, mate. He played for Bristol Rovers between Gretna and Barnsley. Didn't he, Dave?'

'Firstly, I haven't got a clue who you're on about because after the first sentence I suffered a massive overdose of boredom, and secondly I think you are sad and lonely men who have nothing better to do than fiddle with your football yearbooks under your duvets at night.'

'God, and you call yourself a football fan.'

'It's not that, I just think all these stats are boring. I love football because of the drama, the people, the emotion, the camaraderie of being part of something with thousands of other people.'

'Shut up, Dave, you're just weird.'

Attendances are edging up, and before the game kicks off the tone of the crowd is a fraction higher in pitch and volume, driven up by raised aspirations and expectations. We've lost one league game out of the last seventeen, and if we beat the team at the bottom of the table, we go top.

The two tossers behind us have spectacularly failed to catch the wave, however, and I don't think I've ever heard such excruciating, ill-informed bollocks inside a football ground – and anyone who has been to a game anywhere in the world will tell you that excruciating, ill-informed bollocks is in fact the global language of the stadium, so this pair are really going some.

They start whining before we've kicked off, which is merely annoying, but they move effortlessly through the gears to oh-my-god-I-now-know-without-a-shadow-of-a-doubt-that-everyone-is-capable-of-taking-a-human-life stage by about two minutes into the game. They've taken the classic feeder fan/shouter fan routine and taken it to another level.

I glance round at them to confirm I've never seen them before, so they're probably not season ticket holders, but the fact they don't come to the games doesn't stop them foisting their views on everyone else. The older one is the feeder, mumbling something inaudible to the shouter, who then shares his thoughts with everyone within a fifty-foot radius.

'Mumble, grumble, mumble, bumble.'

'I *KNOW*. THAT'S WHAT I'M SAYING. I'VE SAID IT ALL *ALONG*. ALL A-BLOODY LONG! YOU CAN'T PLAY HIM THERE, HE'S OUT OF POSITION! HE'S AN IDIOT! A COMPLETE FUCKING IDIOT AND I'M SICK OF IT! *I* CAN SEE WHAT'S WRONG, WHY CAN'T *HE*, THE BLOODY IDIOT? IDIOT!'

'Mumble, stumble, bumble.'

'I'VE SAID IT FROM DAY ONE, THE TOSSER! HAVEN'T I SAID IT FROM DAY ONE? I'VE SAID IT FROM DAY BLOODY

ONE. HE'S OUT OF POSITION AND HE CAN'T PLAY THERE. HE'S AN IDIOT; I'VE SAID THAT FROM DAY ONE.'

And so on, incessant and unavoidable, ruining everyone else's game because of one man's mistaken belief that we all want to know what he thinks, over and over and over again.

And that's before we go 2-0 down against the team that are bottom of the league. The first goes in on seven minutes, it's two before twenty-five minutes has gone, we're playing atrociously and if that bloke behind me doesn't shut up I swear to God I'm going to kill him with my bare hands, scrambling over the back of my seat to tear his limbs off one by one, wild-eyed and laughing as I beat him to death with his own arm.

I slip into silent despondency, as does nearly everyone else, and you-know-who steps up to the challenge of filling the void admirably. I suppose I must have, but I can't ever remember enjoying a half less.

Football is a truly incredible game. In November, one billion people watched Manchester United play Arsenal. *One billion*. Isn't that amazing? It was beamed into 600 million homes in 202 countries. Land anywhere in the world and within twenty minutes of picking your bags up you could arrange a kickabout with the locals. The whole language of other sports is different – people talk about *following* cricket, but you never hear that applied to football. You can't just follow football, it's impossible. You are led by it, dragged by the nose to Gillingham away on a Tuesday night in January.

There's a very good reason why every other sport pales into insignificance in terms of participation and attendance at matches compared to football – football's a better game, simple as that. It's not because there's a sinister Global Football Marketing Board spending billions to see through its evil plan to crush minority sports for its own financial and political gain – it's just a better game.

Of course there's an obscene amount of money in the game, and no, young lads with millions of pounds in the bank and an NVQ in woodwork often don't make the best role models, but there's a very good reason why there's so much money in football: billions of people are prepared to pay to see games live and on the television. Why? It's just a better game.

Play a beautiful, flowing move in slow motion, put classical music behind it and you will have created a piece of footage which will make the hairs on the back of your neck stand on end. I challenge you to do this with any other sport. It can't be done. Only football can be so aesthetically moving and bring about emotions which are more akin to listening to great music than watching a sport – like I say, it's just a better game.

At least that's how I feel at the moment, but it's easy to wax lyrical when you've just come back from 2-0 down at half-time to win 3-2 and go top of the league.

I don't turn round, but I would love to know how the chuckle brothers behind us greet the goals as we rip Scunthorpe apart. From the moment Lawrence's angled drive hits the back of the net for his tenth league goal of the season, we don't hear another peep out of them. The noise cranks up and ten minutes later Fuller feeds Cresswell to drive home. When Lawrence scores again, it's pandemonium. Unbridled, ecstatic, blissful pandemonium. Slow it down, put it to classical music and enjoy.

When I get home I celebrate with a Jura, which doesn't escape Alison's recently acquired obsession with how much I drink.

'Right, we're going to do an experiment,' she says, and my heart sinks.

'I keep finding empty whisky bottles all over the place and I think we should find out how big the measures you're pouring are.'

'Alison, you found one empty whisky bottle.'

'Exactly. You're obviously getting more cunning.'

'Oh, for God's sake.'

She digs out a measuring cap which came free with a Cypriot bottle of gin years ago and which was put in the drawer reserved for things we will never ever need but which we can't throw away, and tells me to get on with it. It turns out I'm pouring exactly trebles, which I feel quite relieved about, because I thought it was going to be about half a pint. Even Alison seems a bit more relaxed about it, and I curse my lack of ambition at not going for a bit more.

In any case, I tell her, it's not my fault I occasionally endorse alcohol a little over-enthusiastically; it's because I spent so many of my formative years in North Staffordshire. Patiently I explain that, like nearly every city which mushroomed with the Industrial Revolution, Stoke-on-Trent has a long and proud tradition of binge drinking, a culture which becomes even more ingrained with the decline of manufacturing in the area and partly as a result of wages lagging behind pretty much everywhere else in the country. So I'm just reverting to type, I tell her. I have as little control over my habit of drinking to excess every now and then as a savage guard dog starved for three days has over his bite. I am a product of my environment.

It doesn't seem to wash, though, and when she points out both my parents were teachers and I only ever worked in two factories for a total of six weeks, I decide to drop the whole gritty northern thing.

Alcohol can be a wonderful substance, of course, and anyone who says they don't have to drink to have a good time should be treated with a degree of caution until they have proved beyond reasonable doubt they are not religious fundamentalists or dullards. Drink can delight the palate, it boosts confidence, eases awkward social occasions, complements fine food and of course helps to steady the shakes just before operating dangerous machinery.

But I'm the first to admit it can lead to problems, and not just the run-of-the-mill hangover, casual violence, unhygienic sexual acts behind a nightclub, arguing with your mates and generally acting like an arse sort of problems. Public health leaders in Stoke-on-Trent have made tackling alcohol dependency and alcohol abuse a priority because of their impact on life expectancy, crime rates, limbs being lopped off by dangerous machinery and unplanned pregnancies.

So according to the figures, if it's another child we're after then we should be going clubbing and getting absolutely mullered every single night – we'd be proud expectant parents again in no time. Admittedly, Alison might be expecting the offspring of someone called Spliff, and I might have got the girl from the call centre (now wrinkled to leather and toothless) up the duff but, hey, it's a start.

A few days after the Scunthorpe game I spot something which suggests all the eminent doctors, therapists, economists and social engineers drafted in to curb drinking in the city could be fighting a losing battle.

'Drinkers hope to stop health centre,' says the headline in *The Sentinel*. Now if I was the director of public health in Stoke-on-Trent reading that, and my juicy bonus depended on promoting the benefits of a healthy lifestyle over booze-fuelled hedonism I'd either pack my bags and become a GP in the Cotswolds or I'd go for the 'if you can't beat them join them' option and start drinking myself into an early grave.

The story is basically about a pub in Meir which the authorities want to bulldoze to make way for a health centre – an uplifting, optimistic symbol made physical of the city's determination to rise from its alcohol-stewed past to a bright new dawn of well-being, where whole estates turn out at 6.30 a.m. for communal neighbourhood aerobics and everyone cycles to work at the muesli plant, you might think.

Or not. Regulars and locals have formed an action group to stop this wanton act of vandalism by the stormtroopers of the nanny state. I imagine them congregating outside the Kings Arms, ringleaders whipping them into a frenzy and then all of them marching on the local GP's surgery brandishing pitchforks and burning torches.

'Burn them! Burn them!'

'We want beer! We want beer!'

'You are the disease! We are the cure! You are the disease! We are the cure!'

'Run them out of town! Hang them from the lampposts with their own stethoscopes!'

'I need a drink!'

And so on. In fairness, it transpires they don't actually want to kill anyone who gets between them and a pint; they just think the pub is an important part of the community and they want the health centre to be built somewhere nearby. I can see their point – it turns out the Kings Arms has nine bowling teams, two darts teams, two cricket teams, snooker teams and a crib team. By the sounds of it, if the place closes, the streets of Meir will become a no-go zone for teenagers as gangs of pensioners with nothing left to do but fight and steal cars scuff around outside the shopping centre, ruining their health with strong cider and alcopops.

Less than a week after the Scunthorpe match we beat Ipswich 1-0 at home and we're top of the table with sixty-two points, Bristol are second on sixty-one and Watford are third with sixty. It's been a good few weeks.

CHAPTER 17

The way I feel at the moment, I'm not even certain I can inflict being a Stoke fan on Harry, let alone another as yet unborn child. I'm reminded of Philip Larkin's *This Be The Verse*:

> They fuck you up, your mum and dad.
> They may not mean to, but they do.
> They fill you with the faults they had
> And add some extra, just for you.

Actually, I'm not reminded of it at all, to be honest. I looked up 'mum and dad' in a book of quotations and I thought it would make me sound clever. While I'm at it, another one I liked was Oscar Wilde's:

> Children begin by loving their parents; after a time they judge them; rarely, if ever, do they forgive them.

It sounded somehow appropriate when I was thinking about how much it could screw Harry's life up if I insist on moulding him into a Stoke fan.

Just over a week ago we were top of the table, we'd lost one league game in sixteen, optimism and excitement were running high and home crowds were starting to break through the twenty thousand barrier. Since then, we've lost 2-0 away at Preston and 3-0 away at QPR, when we were truly terrible – slow, unimaginative and weak. Rangers have eleven on-target goal attempts, compared to our two, and it's a miracle we didn't go down by a bigger margin. Just before half-time, Andy Griffin is sent off as a result of one of the most laughable refereeing decisions in the history of English football, but there's no way we would have got anything from the game; we're already 2-0 down and chasing the ball like schoolboys.

The good news is the game is on the telly, so the general national uproar about the sending off means it will just be a formality to have the red card overturned by the FA. The bad news is the game is on the telly, so every man and his dog feels compelled to lap up and regurgitate the usual lines about the uncouth long-ball merchants finally getting their comeuppance at the hands of their stylish opponents.

Is it right to lead Harry gently by the hand towards a lifetime of disappointment, frustration and ridicule from his mates in Man United, Chelsea and Arsenal shirts? I don't think I've got any choice. I will probably tell myself it is morally right for people to support their local clubs, although I'm not sure I could make a convincing argument for it, but footballing allegiance – like a tendency for temper tantrums or a genetic predisposition to baldness – is probably just one more flaw we pass on to our kids without premeditation and almost without noticing.

I can't think of a more effective way of losing my hero status with Harry than making him sit through Stoke against Bury on a Tuesday night in February, although I'm sure he will have realised I'm not the ideal person to put your faith in long before it gets to that point. At the moment he couldn't think more of me if I was President of the Known Universe, although a fireman would probably knock me into a cocked hat.

Every day there are sobering reminders of how important I am to his life. When he calls out 'Daddy!' in his sleep, or when he comes on the phone at work and says 'Daddy come see Harry now?' Or when I go to nursery to pick him up and he's so overjoyed to see me he sprints across the room, pushing babies out of the way, trampling on delicate hands and toes and kneeing little girls in the face in his rush to get to me.

Like I say, I'm his hero, and the pride I feel as a result of that is almost certainly partly down to machismo and biological conditioning. ('Me man. Me impregnate woman and give baby.') Having said that, when he's sitting on my knee and he starts prodding my slack man-breasts and saying 'Boobies, daddy, boobies,' the feeling that I could quite comfortably wrestle sabre-toothed tigers and slay woolly mammoths with my bare hands fades pretty rapidly, but I suppose you have to take the rough with the smooth.

The truth is, I love being a dad and I love my son unequivocally and completely; both of which mean I'm one of the most satisfied men in the world. If I had another child I may actually be *the* most satisfied man in the world, but I genuinely don't mind either way.

From the second I took Harry from the nurse's hands, wrapped in hospital regulation towels (Harry, not the nurse, although she may have been wrapped in towels, I can't remember – perhaps she was going to a toga party afterwards) everything changed. Not in a dramatic, seismic, romantic way, but without noticing and without effort I sidestepped into a world where everything was slightly – but fundamentally – different.

For me, the pleasure in being a father is at least partly selfish. Two-and-a-half years on, I sometimes still forget I have a child, because I will walk into a room and I will see, say, Harry's fire engine on the sofa, and for a split second I will be absolutely thrown by how such an incongruous object could be in my lounge. A millisecond later, when my two worlds realign, the feeling is almost exactly the same as when that nurse, perhaps impatient to get to her toga party, passed me my son. It cuts through all the froth, the flannel and the fug and makes me realise with absolutely unfettered, blue-skied winter's day clarity what's important.

Only since Harry has been born have I genuinely forgiven myself for hurting so many people so deeply so often, for being such a self-centred tosser and for being such an appalling son.

Here's a list of some of the things I've done over the years that I'm ashamed of.

1. Not called my mum and dad for months at a time. This must be pretty common in blokes, though, and I'm getting much better at it, so it probably only rates a six on the patented Ima Tosser index of shame.
2. Arranging a weekend away in Cornwall with my mates, telling them they could stay at my nan's and then deciding to go to Scotland with a different set of mates. I didn't tell my nan that 20 people were going to land on her doorstep and I didn't tell my mates I wasn't going to turn up either, so that's probably a seven.
3. Taking money from a charity box. I know, I know, but I was very young, so it's probably just a seven as well.
4. At school, deliberately tripping up the kid who must have felt sick with worry, continuously, for five years of his life, for fear of what he was going to have to go through before he could reach the sanctuary of his home. I couldn't stand bullies even at school, but just this once, almost instinctively, I stuck my foot out for the cheap laugh. Maybe a six.
5. Taking part in daily baguette attacks when I was working in France. We were cleaning tents for an English holiday company and we had one of those vans with the sliding door on the side. Every morning we'd go to the bakery to get a load of bread for the whole crew. On the way back we'd drive round, sometimes for up to an hour, until we saw a cyclist. We'd approach him slowly from behind,

114

the designated person would slide open the door, hold on with one hand, lean out and, as we drew alongside, hit the cyclist on the back of the head with a baguette, leaving him astonished and wobbling in our wake. The potential for serious injury or death should make this a nine or a ten, but we only went slowly, we didn't hit them full force – just enough to put a forty-five degree bend in the bread – and I'm pretty sure the worst one of our victims suffered was crust shrapnel. In addition, we could have used much more dangerous baked products: a rock-hard crusted farmhouse loaf would have been lethal, for example, while a bap, a bloomer or a floury batch would have meant we would have had to drive much closer to the cyclist. You can't beat a baguette for reach, so that's probably a seven.

6. Agreeing to buy a house with my then girlfriend, seeing a financial adviser together and applying for a joint mortgage. I failed to tell her I had bought a house on my own a few weeks before because I knew the relationship was doomed. That remarkable display of heartless cowardice must rank as an eight or a nine, with ten being reserved for serial killers, those particularly loathsome men who take pretend cricket shots or golf swings when they're standing around the office and people who use punctuation marks to put smiley faces or winking faces – or, let's face it, any sort of face at all – at the end of text messages or emails.

There are more, of course, and many of them much more shameful, but since Harry was born I feel at ease with myself, as if I've redressed the balance of the cosmic karma by contributing to him being around, paid my debt to society with interest, taken out a cash ISA for a major charity, ticked the gift aid box and donated funds for a new bench to be put up in the park.

All this is extremely useful and liberating, of course,

because psychologically it pretty much gives me carte blanche to carry on being an infuriating, self-centred tosser, safe in the knowledge that my karmaccount is still healthily in credit.

Another of the strange effects of becoming a father is that I have become disturbingly morbid. Maybe it's the whole birth and death, Yin and Yang, as something is created so something is destroyed thing. Or maybe it's just because I'm getting old and my subconscious is preparing me for the unavoidable slide into ill-health, senility and oblivion.

I find myself luxuriating in a variety of melancholic, death-related fantasies: Alison dies and Harry and I forge a beautiful lifelong bond from the adversity, pain and mutual dependency; Harry dies, Alison doesn't admit it, but she blames me and leaves, I move to Cornwall with the express intention of becoming an alcoholic, sitting day after day staring out to sea from the window of the Ship Inn, drinking myself into the grave within a year; or I die, and, well, that's about as far as I get with that one because I'm dead.

I imagine the events leading up to my death quite a lot as well. I'll hear something on the car radio about a pile-up on the motorway and I start imagining what would happen to Harry if I died. Maybe he'd go off the rails because of the lack of a father figure and end up a crack addict forging his mother's signature on cheques to fund his habit; or perhaps the subconscious scar left by the demise of someone he doesn't even remember would spur him on to incredible achievements – 'I dedicate my tenth Olympic gold to the man I never knew; I did it all for you, Dad.' That sort of thing. I try to avoid playing the most likely outcome in my head (that my passing has absolutely no impact on him at all, that he becomes a well-rounded, normal bloke, largely because he almost immediately considers the guy Alison shacks up with a couple of weeks after the funeral to be his dad and it turns out he's a pretty decent cove and a much better father figure than I could ever be) for obvious reasons.

I quite enjoy watching my funeral, as if I'm floating above the proceedings, dipping in and out of speeches and conversations. My teary wife telling Harry to always remember what a good father I was and that no-one could ever take my place. Snatches of conversation between mourners ('He was so intelligent and he'd do anything for anyone.' 'Yes, and it was strange – even though he was short, a bit overweight and going bald, there was just something about him. He was very desirable.' 'That's so true. I used to fantasise about him constantly.')

I usually shake myself from this macabre daydream when Alison's on her fifth large white and getting too close to that suave git who hasn't even bothered to wear black. Almost inevitably, when I come to I'm about to plough into the back of a bus and the prospect of an early grave seems much less appealing.

Another alarming result of becoming a father (or at least of *me* becoming a father; I wouldn't entirely rule out the possibility that I'm just a bit weird) is that I find the strangest things move me to tears: songs by Enrique Iglesias and Ronan Keating can make me blubber uncontrollably, and if I hear *Suffer Little Children* by The Smiths, I more often than not have to book the following day off work. Wildlife documentaries are a killer, and if they show young animals (even insects, for God's sake) being eaten or losing their parents, I surreptitiously have to push back in the sofa, tilt my head up and open my eyes wide to make sure a stray tear doesn't escape.

Thinking about it, maybe that's why I can't turn the pages of a newspaper any more without licking my fingers. Maybe all the moisture has been diverted to storage reservoirs connected to my tear ducts.

About three months into the pregnancy, Alison calls to me from the bathroom. She's sitting on the toilet pouring blood and she looks at me with all the grief and fear the world could possibly hold.

'I've lost it,' she says.

I can't remember how we get there, but soon we're in the doctor's office and she's telling us it's quite possible that we've lost our baby; that this little embryo, which had against all the odds started to unfurl, unseen, into life, could have been flushed away with the rest of the bright pink froth. Up until then I thought I'd been pretty ambivalent about having kids. Yes, I was happy we were having a baby, but it wouldn't have bothered me, I thought, if it had never happened. Bits of my world started to crumble round the edges as I listened to that kind, gentle doctor, and I was no longer under any illusion about how desperately I wanted to meet the strange little being who I sang the same song to every morning, my mouth brushing Alison's stomach.

We had to go to the hospital, it took an age to get a scan, but then there he was, happy as Harry, little heart going ten to the dozen.

Maybe I'm over-dramatising it. Years ago, when it was common for women to have a dozen babies, but for only a few of them to survive past the age of two, I'm pretty sure the father-to-be didn't pace the room wringing his hands because his wife passed a bit of blood. He probably slapped her around a bit; told her to pull herself together and get the tea on the table.

Life must have been unimaginably stark in places like the Potteries as the Industrial Revolution gathered pace, and even now infant mortality rates here are still among the highest in the country. When Harry was first born I used to wheel him around Hartshill Cemetery in the pram, figure-of-eighting on the broad tracks under the trees. There's a section given over to children, some who died just a few weeks old, and the poems inscribed on the headstones, and the shrines of bright plastic toys and mouldy teddy bears, break your heart.

The relief and joy I felt when the doctor finally confirmed our baby was still alive was remarkable and every time I squeaked the pram past one of those tragic little memorials in the cemetery I couldn't help feeling blessed that the only lasting physical reminder of our own meaningless, thousand-a-day trauma, was a small, fading bloodstain the shape of Cyprus on the bathroom carpet.

CHAPTER 18

One of the best things about having a kid, of course, is it completely changes the way you row with your wife.

Without us noticing, Harry has turned into an indispensable channel for constructive disagreement, and his very presence in the room is a calming and civilising influence conducive to diplomatic negotiation.

Before Harry was born, a typical argument might go something like this:

'Have you heard the sound that dishwasher's making? You've put forks in the wrong way round again, haven't you? Why don't you listen to a word I say? You're a bloody idiot.'

'Will you just shut the ... shut up about the dishwasher? On and on and bloody on. Just give it a rest or I'll smash the things to pieces with my pestle. Or mortar. I've forgotten which is which again.'

Or:

'God, you're so untidy.'

'Blah, blah, bloody blah.'

Both of which are admirably to the point, but they're not going to win any awards for intelligent reasoning.

For the last two years, though, we have become masters at circumspect criticism, safe in the knowledge the other person won't lose their temper in case the books are right and raised voices at this critical stage of Harry's development cripple him emotionally, leading in later life to an inability to commit, poor concentration, drug addiction, recidivism, psychopathic tendencies and tennis elbow.

Now a typical argument might be:

'Oh, Harry, what's that sound?'

'What sound dat, Mummy?'

'It's the dishwasher, isn't it? Can you hear it? Clank, clunk, clank, clunk.'

'Cank, cunk.'

'That's right, Harry, good boy! I wonder why it's making that noise, Harry. Is it because Daddy is incompetent? Can you say in-com-pe-tent?'

'Silly Daddy.'

'That's close enough, darling, well done.'

'Oh, Harry,' I counter, 'can you tell me what this is? It's a pan, isn't it? Shall we ask Mummy why the pan is still here?'

'Why pan, Mummy?'

'Is it because Mummy says it takes up too much room in the dishwasher and because she refuses to put the dishwasher on twice a day because of the environment?'

'Viroment, Daddy.'

'Do you think we should tell Mummy that she already kills five thousand fish a week by pouring bleach down the toilet and sinks three times a day and she personally contributes five tonnes of landfill a year because she can't fight her compulsion to buy disposable antiseptic wipes, disposable anti-static wipes, disposable toddler wipes or in fact disposable wipes of any sort? I don't know what I see in her, Harry, I really don't.'

'Boobies, Daddy, boobies.'

Or:

'Oh, Harry, what a mess! Do you think your daddy will ever put away that tie?'

'Shall I tell Mummy I will put away my tie when she moves the wedge of receipts that have been in the fruit bowl for three years?'

'We like to be organised, don't we, Harry? We may need those receipts some day.'

'Hey, Harry, shall we tell Mummy we may need haemorrhoid cream some day as well, but we wouldn't put it in the fruit bowl?'

'Oh, Harry, your daddy really is a p-r-i-c-k, isn't he?'

The two demoralising defeats against Preston and QPR mean we slip to second place, clinging on to an automatic ticket to the promised land by our broken, grubby, unfashionable long-ball fingernails. But we've played a match more than nearly everyone else now, and all our main rivals play their games in hand on Tuesday.

So, as of 7.30pm Tuesday, this is how it stands: Bristol City are top with sixty-four points, we're second with sixty-two, Watford are third on sixty-one and West Brom are in fourth on fifty-eight. I turn on the radio and pray for them all to lose.

Bristol and Watford draw, but West Brom, the spawny gits, beat Sheffield Wednesday with a goal five minutes into injury time. So we're down to third, behind Watford on goal difference and out of the automatic promotion places.

The results could have been a lot worse for us, but I'm nervous that the bubble has burst, the fragile mortar bonding the fans is going to crumble away before it has a chance to set and the players' confidence will shrivel and die under the heat of the national spotlight. We need a win on Saturday at home to Burnley. *I* need a win against Burnley on Saturday, to fan the faith into flame again and allow me to look forward to games with excitement once more, not this nagging doubt and dread.

On the walk to the ground my blind optimism returns, but it soon retreats as the game gets underway. The players are nervous and most of the eighteen thousand-plus fans are nervous. From the off we look out of sorts. Within minutes

Carlo Nash, who we've just signed on loan from Wigan, has been beaten far too easily at the near post after some bloody woeful defending and we're 1-0 down. I'll spare you the sordid details of the rest of the game, but a deep gloom washes over me, seeping deeper with each minute.

Ade Akinbiyi, a former hero at the Brit, misses a three-yard toe-poke to make it 2-0. After that, Burnley shut up shop, content to hang on for the win, but we don't look like we'd score if we played until Tuesday.

I know I get over-dramatic in these situations, but this is it – the dream's over. We'll slip down the table and, come May, miss out on a play-off place by a fraction and I try to convince myself that this season, no matter where we end up, will have surpassed all expectations. What else did I expect? A season that ends with the eyes of the nation on my club and my city as we win a promotion worth £60m? Stupid, childish, pointless, energy-sapping dreams.

As the clock flicks to ninety minutes, just as I'm entering my weepy nadir, a through ball touches off Fuller's forehead, Cresswell gets behind the defenders and races towards goal. As he heads towards goal, a challenge comes in and he buckles. Is it a penalty? I don't know and I don't give a toss, because the ref's pointing towards the spot. We're up; dancing, cheering, hugging each other, before it dawns on all of us at pretty much the same time that someone has still got to put the ball in the back of the net. We'll miss; I know we will. This is Stoke and they can't help but let me down again. It's nothing personal, it's just what they do. The tension is painful.

About forty yards in front of me, Lawrence sets off on one of the longest run-ups for a penalty I've ever seen. Here he comes, gathering speed, swinging his right foot back and ... stepping over the ball.

It's all I can do to stop myself clambering over people's backs, onto the pitch and beating the flouncy-haired tosser to a bloody slurry for making me go through this again. He traipses back to re-start his run-up, gather speed, swing his right foot back and …

There follows a series of sounds that never quite catch up with what my eyes are seeing, which, in turn, lag behind, or maybe race ahead of, the information my brain is processing. I later work out that the sharp smack/thud is the ball hitting the post, the softer slap/thud is the ball hitting the keeper on his back on the rebound and the hollow thunk/thud is the bloke behind me's fist smashing into my head as he erupts with ecstasy as the ball crosses the line.

Pandemonium ensues. I look around as we're all in mid-mental and everyone's got those fluid, uncontrolled and uncontrollable expressions that you only see on and around a football pitch. Strange, wonderful gurnings borne out of the incapacity of physical beings to express the explosion of joy, relief and excitement that a vital goal brings and the semi-formed comprehension that what you've just seen could help change your life forever.

It's the same utterly untrammelled orgasmic cocktail that sends players or sometimes managers careering around the ground as if pissed-up leprechauns have taken control of their limbs when a particularly important goal is scored or the final whistle means a championship, a promotion or an escape from relegation by the narrowest of squeaks.

It's not a great result and it's not a great performance, but Bristol play out a goalless draw with Leicester and Watford and West Brom don't play. Somehow, we're back up to second.

Depending on which minute you ask me I'm either convinced this is our season and we're going up, or I know with absolute certainty we are going to snatch defeat from the jaws of victory once again, start the usual slide down the rankings and miss out on the play-offs by three or four points.

Just before the Norwich game I see an article in the

Telegraph which sways me back to the belief that the planets are aligning in our favour. Apparently an analysis of English league results since the Second World War shows teams who wear predominantly red strips win more points a game and finish higher in the league on average than teams who wear other colours.

Scientists (they're scientists in the *Telegraph*; in *The Sun* they would be boffins, or possibly even egg-heads) believe the colour gives a team an advantage because, subconsciously, opponents associate it with aggression and dominance and therefore they become more defensive.

In the article, the lead author of the research, Professor Martin Attrill of the School of Biological Sciences at the University of Plymouth, says: 'Previous evidence from studies of combat sports and psychological tests suggest that competitors wearing red perform better than average.

'It is believed that colour can stimulate deep-rooted aggression and dominance in competitive situations. Similarly research shows players who encounter opponents in red display more defensive reactions.'

Suddenly, I remember the glorious, all-conquering Madeley High School team of 1980/1981 of which I was a part. The shirts we wore were ... deep, vibrant, aggressive, dominant red. And, less importantly, England won the 1966 World Cup wearing ... red!

Then I think of the phrases to see red and to feel the red mist come down. Of course, it all starts to make sense. Even the fact that half the time we're really good and half the time we're completely bloody hopeless can be explained – we wear red and white *stripes*. Half the strip is namby pamby, wishy washy, curl-up-in-a-ball, I surrender *white*.

Growing in confidence, I read on.

They also studied local rivals where one team plays in red and the other doesn't – Stoke and Port Vale, Liverpool and Everton, Manchester United and Manchester City, Nottingham Forest and Notts County, Bristol City and Bristol Rovers, Arsenal and Spurs, Millwall and Charlton and Sheffield United and Sheffield Wednesday – and in every case except Sheffield the red team performed better over the period.

The fact that teams who usually wear red strips perform no better than teams who wear other colours when they have to switch to their non-red away kit clinches it for me.

Co-author Dr Russell Hill, from Durham University, said: 'The influx of wealthy foreign owners has changed the resources available to some teams and this should result in increased success, regardless of their shirt colour.

'Nevertheless, in close matches where teams are evenly balanced, we still predict that wearing red could tip the balance between success and failure and the red advantage will still persist.'

That's it then. Bristol will go up as champions because they wear all red and we'll just squeeze up in second because of those treacherous white stripes. Watford and West Brom will stutter and stall, dragged down the table by the sheer weight of their failure-coloured kit.

I'm in the process of emailing Tony Pulis to tell him to whip up to Partners to get a couple of red highlighters and give them to Pericard to fill in the stripes (after all, he'll be used to doing mundane jobs like that from prison) when a terrible thought strikes me. What about Charlton? They play in solid red shirts and at the moment they're in fifth place. That means they could beat us to second place. Having said that, I figure, we would probably be the only team in the play-offs wearing predominantly red, so I'm pretty sure we would go up eventually.

Then I wonder why we have been wallowing in the lower divisions for twenty-three years if these boffins (scientists, my arse) are so clever, and I decide to do some research of my own.

I find out the following national teams have a significant amount of red in their strips.

São Tomé and Príncipe. Removed from the FIFA world ranking lists because they haven't played enough games. They withdrew from the 1994 World Cup, didn't enter the 1998 World Cup, didn't qualify for the World Cups in 2002 and 2006 and they have withdrawn from the 2010 World Cup.

American Samoa. Ranked equal 202 – currently the lowest possible placing – in the FIFA table. In 2001, American Samoa were beaten 31-0 by Australia, the biggest defeat in international footballing history. (Those bloody Australians. How ruthlessly competitive do you have to be to keep smacking them in at a rate of one every three minutes after you get to, say, 10-0?) Duane Atualeveo is their top scorer ever with a majestic three goals. Having said that, that's a bloody sight more than big Mama's got this season.

Anguilla. Ranked equal 202. Several of the current squad play for Slough Town.

Montserrat. Ranked equal 202. Although in fairness, since 1995 they have only played a handful of matches, most away from home, because of volcanic activity on the island. I'm presuming the streams of lava were undaunted by – or redder than – Montserrat's kit.

Timor-Leste (nickname: The Rising Sun). Ranked equal 202. If Wikipedia is to be believed, the only person to have ever scored for Timor-Leste is Emilio Da Silva, although in mitigation of the rest of the team, they've only played a handful of games since they were formed in 2005 and they still have scoring rates comparable to some Championship strikers I could name.

I'm hoping it's just a coincidence, but all these teams seem to be coached by Englishmen (including former Stoke hero Mark Chamberlain) or people who played in the English leagues.

I'm fairly certain the modest success of these teams is probably due to factors other than kit colour, such as poverty, having a national population of three or living on the slopes of one of the world's most active volcanoes, but my confidence in the red shirt theory is starting to falter.

Further investigations reveal British forces were wearing red when they crossed the ford at Rorke's Drift in 1879 expecting to meet little resistance from the Zulus. They were wrong and they were soon all but wiped out by Zulu warriors ('tharsands of 'em.') in one of the most infamous defeats in British military history. I'm not sure what kit the Zulus were wearing, but I don't think it was red.

Also, I could be wrong, but I'm pretty sure the *Titanic* was painted red below the waterline. I decide not to put too much faith in the whole red strip thing.

CHAPTER 19

Here's a list of things I can no longer do since I turned forty.

1. Understand the endings of *Lewis*. Or any other detective shows for that matter. I'm okay for probably the first twenty minutes, then over the next twenty minutes I become increasingly confused, and by the time Lewis explains how the eccentric academic actually *wasn't* dead when he was placed in the shallow grave and something about people having their watches and all the clocks in their houses changed, he might as well be talking in an incredibly rare Korean dialect with a pair of socks stuffed in his mouth. My brain is rapidly stiffening up, unable to make those natural agile leaps it used to take in its stride. I'm even struggling with *Midsomer Murders*, for God's sake, although, assuming they haven't all been butchered in episodes of *Lewis*, there are Oxford academics without the necessary IQ to make the leaps of logic and belief needed to enjoy John Nettles sniffing around villages which seem to be made entirely of thatched cottages. They're a bloody fire hazard those Midsomer villages, I tell you, especially since the smoking ban. All it would take is one carelessly discarded fag end outside The Ram's Scrotum and the whole place would be up like a tinderbox.

   Anyway, as I say, *Lewis* is beyond me and I fear the onset of premature senility. Grace, my mother-in-law, has to explain the endings to me, and she's about twenty-five years older than me. She is also the only person I know outside the animated world who has actually slipped on a banana skin, so you can understand why I find it alarming she is more mentally agile than me. If she can be brought to ground by fruit peel, what hope have I got?

Another symptom of my descent into dementia is an inability to grasp the implications of other results on Stoke's position in the table. At the game, Robbo can reel off every possible permutation for the next three weeks, but I have to write it down at work, or jot notes beside the tables in the paper.

I don't know anyone, however, who has gone as far as Ian. A few weeks ago he devised some sort of computer programme which analyses form and predicts finishing positions of all the clubs involved in the promotion race.

For the first three Mondays after he developed the system he emailed us all amended forecasts based on the weekend results, although he has since stopped in the face of severe piss-taking.

2. Turn pages without licking my fingers. (See previous chapters.)

3. Put on a duvet cover. Okay, I was never going to win any awards for this before I turned forty, but I've definitely got worse at it. I despise this job, and I do anything to get out of it. It's a Sunday night chore, so I'm usually already contemplating self-harm to balance the pain of chucking away another hour of my life failing to understand *Lewis*.

I've even tried the classic schoolboy trick of pretending to be ill.

'I'm just not feeling at my best, darling. You do the duvet cover and I'll put on the pillowcases.'

'How do you mean, not well?'

'I just feel really achy. I feel as if by tomorrow there are going to be doctors crawling all over me, scratching their heads in amazement that I'm still alive.'

'Just put the bloody duvet cover on and stop skiving.'

'Look, love,' I implore, 'people are just good at different

things, and sometimes you have to accept that. You're good at putting duvet covers on and I'm good at brushing my teeth.'

And it's *true*. I *am* much better at brushing my teeth than Alison. She's useless at it. I don't mean she doesn't brush them properly, I just mean her technique is poor and as a consequence she finds it impossible to retain the toothpaste in her mouth while she's brushing.

From the moment the toothbrush hits her mouth there is a constant river of minty lather pouring over her lower lip, down her chin and into the sink. I could be wrong, but I'm sure on occasions it comes down her nose as well. And possibly out of her eyes. If you've ever seen one of those documentaries about bullfighting, where the poor creature is on its last legs, with swords sticking out of it at all angles and bilious curtains of pink saliva hanging from its mouth, you'll get the picture. Especially when she's got a touch of gum disease.

I, on the other hand, am the tidiest tooth brusher I know. I can walk from room to room cleaning my teeth without spilling a drop, and I admit I often do this just to annoy my sink-bound wife.

'Olé!' I cry, as I spit my toothpaste out in triumph. Like I say, people are just good at different things.

4. Drink heavily. Or, in fact, moderately. (See previous chapters and, in all likelihood, later chapters.)

5. Urinate standing up. Okay, I can do it if I have to but, given the choice, I'll pee like a girl every time – it's just nice to have a sit down.

6. Go straight to bed. Before I turned forty I would have my tea, watch a bit of telly and go to bed. Simple. With a quick stop to have a wash and wander ostentatiously from room to room brushing my teeth, it was sofa to pillow in sub-two minutes.

Nowadays it seems I have to start preparations as soon as

the washing up is done if I want to be in bed before two in the morning. For some reason I now get paranoid that I'm going to forget something vital for work so I make a little pile of things for the morning – car keys, mobile phone, some fruit and so on. Then I have to get a glass of water, having already succumbed to the pensioner's inability to contemplate a good night's rest without one.

In the bathroom, there has to be a masochistic inspection of the consequences of being another day older. I stand sideways on, relax my stomach and make the nightly vow to get some exercise in a bid to halt my gut's migration out and down and to shrink my man-boobs from a C cup to a B cup. Finally, it's a scrabble through my bedside drawers to make sure the heartburn medicine is still nestled in my socks.

7. Load a dishwasher. (See previous chapters, and, I have no doubt, future chapters.) Strictly speaking, I don't know if I'm any worse at this since I turned forty, because we haven't had one that long, but if Alison's to be believed, I am truly a dishwasher-loading dunce. My latest misdemeanour is to put plastic chopping boards too close together.

'The water and detergent won't be able to get between them and clean them properly,' I'm told.

'But it's water. How big do you think water molecules are – the size of a potato? Water gets into microscopic fissures in rocks, eventually forging huge cracks; it seeps through the tiniest spaces imaginable and in fact it passes through seemingly solid substances like paper. But if you're telling me red-hot water forced out under pressure will give up the ghost at a centimetre gap between two chopping boards, then so be it.'

'Don't start all that geology crap again, just shift the bloody board.'

Since Labour came to power in 1997, they have reportedly introduced more than 3,000 new laws. I don't know if

Alison modelled her approach to dishwasher logistics on Blair and Brown's enthusiasm for rules and red tape, or vice versa, but either way it's not making my life any easier.

8. Imagine Stoke doing anything even vaguely interesting. (See previous chapters, but in real danger of needing revision if we beat Norwich tonight.)

It's Norwich away on a Tuesday night. Pulis has dropped Fuller, our top scorer and undoubtedly our most talented player. That means we have Cresswell and Sidibe up front. Sidibe, the lethal goal machine who has scored a grand total of one goal in twenty-nine appearances as the season draws to a close. I'm listening on the radio, and Norwich are all over us. Ten minutes into the second half, Rory Delap hurls in a trademark long throw, Sidibe gets a head to it and doubles his league goals tally as the ball loops over the Norwich keeper and into the back of the net. We hang on for dear life and we're second behind Bristol with Watford in third.

CHAPTER 20

Watford away. Watford, who were in the Premier League last season. Watford, who have been top or close to it all this season. Watford, who have been vilified with almost as much hysteria as we have this season. Watford, who are just three points behind us with a game in hand. Everyone's calling it a 'six-pointer' or a 'mustn't lose', which isn't strictly accurate because all the clubs toward the top are doing their utmost not to get promoted and falling over themselves to help everyone else out.

All the same, it's an incredibly important game, and I can't remember feeling this nervous about football for years. In your average, nothing-to-play-for season, I might start to have a twinge of excitement about the next game on the Friday afternoon, maybe Thursday if there's the added bonus of going for a few beers after the game to look forward to. But now every match we play comes with the weight of implication and a dread which swells from the Monday, grows daily and breaks at 3 p.m. on Saturday.

Some swanky firm of accountants has estimated promotion to the Premier League is worth more than £60 million to the successful clubs. That makes the Watford game easily the most nauseatingly critical match since at least the play-off semi-final that would have seen us back in the top division twelve years ago.

Which is why looking for kitchen appliances and worktops on the morning of the game is filling me with even less delight than it would in normal circumstances. Difficult to imagine, I know.

Alison seems to have overcome her fears about granite

being only fractionally more hardy than crystal fashioned by the world's finest craftsmen. A product only a few months ago deemed too delicate for the dishwasher is now the only material which will do for our work surfaces. Now, granite is to be trusted to withstand red-hot pans being placed on it, heavy objects being dropped on it by accident and the overzealous use of an impressive array of implements designed for cutting, crushing, mashing and pulverising.

Given her concerns earlier in the year about the porosity of granite, I consider asking her how she is going to stop spilt gravy from seeping through the worktop and – rather like the goo in the *Alien* movies – dripping in a distinctly unhygienic fashion into the cupboards below.

Instinct tells me not to press ahead with my undoubtedly hilarious and unchallengeable observations in a showroom full of implements designed for cutting, crushing, mashing and pulverising.

I'm also slightly concerned that, gram for gram, granite appears to be a shade more expensive than platinum.

'Don't worry,' Alison says. 'We'll get it from the undertaker.'

Twenty minutes later and I'm parking up in a yard filled with granite gravestones. The whole place looks a bit like a Scooby Doo location, but it turns out this firm of monumental stonemasons does a sideline in kitchen work surfaces. Fair play to them, they're a fraction of the cost of the big shops, but I've just got this nagging worry it'll turn up with some sort of grim inscription on it.

'Here lies Bob Machin. Aged 46. He loved a fag.

'Beloved husband and father, heroic leader of the Meir anti-health centre uprisings.'

All very touching, but you don't really want to chop your cucumber on it.

Eight games to go.

After twenty-two minutes, the almost-universally-reviled

Rob Styles sends off John Eustace, our former hero. Pulis seems to think this is exactly the situation in which to cling on for a point for seventy minutes, and for the rest of the game we fail to even look like scoring against Watford's ten men. They have ten goal attempts; we have three.

In the second half, Styles excels himself and gives Watford a penalty for a handball which no-one else in the ground sees, but Carlo Nash makes a brilliant save and we survive. Amazingly, the point is enough to take us back to the top of the table.

A dark cloud is spreading from the horizon like an approaching sandstorm or toxic smoke, something so awful I have so far avoided mentioning it. The implications are just too horrible to face square-on. Someone – and I will spare their blushes with anonymity – has booked a holiday for the extended family in the same week as the play-off finals. If the holiday had been down south somewhere, or anywhere in the UK for that matter, it would have been all right. We could quite happily drive to Wembley from John o'Groats if necessary. But no. This particular party of ten – five of whom are Stoke City season ticket holders – are going to Menorca for the week. Now don't get me wrong; I'm not ungrateful. I'm sure Menorca is a lovely place, with a stunning coastline, beautiful, crystal-clear blue seas, friendly locals, excellent cuisine, a rich and varied culture and wall-to-wall sunshine. But it's not Wembley Stadium if your team is appearing there in the play-off finals with the chance to make the top division for the first time in more than two decades.

The booking is an error on a par with the greatest blunders of modern times, including Neville Chamberlain waving that piece of paper around in 1938 bragging about peace for our time just before it all kicked off good-style, the bloke from Decca records who turned down the Beatles because 'guitar groups are out of fashion', Vincent Pericard's decision to say his step-dad was driving the car, and Peter Coates when he said 'Okay, Tony, you've sold him to me. Let's buy Jon Parkin.'

CHAPTER 21

I love the drive over to Sheffield. Within minutes of leaving home, the car's winding and climbing into the Peak District. Impractically-shaped fields are marked out with shining, sodden, fallen-down dry stone walls and the twisted, stunted trees are straight out of a horror film. I wouldn't be surprised to see the bloke from the monumental stonemasons standing by the side of the road, blank eye sockets following me as he waves in slow motion and the opening credits roll. As the car levels out on the high moors, the dark grey sky looks so low I half expect to see it swirling madly in the rear view mirror, disturbed by our passage just inches below. The wide horizon is a strip of beautiful, washed-out brightness silhouetting abandoned farm buildings and distant escarpments.

Every few feet, shredded plastic bags caught in the barbed wire lining the road are snapping in the fierce wind. Most of them must have been clinging there for years, by the looks of it, bleached, washed and battered to white by the elements.

I love the northern upland place names, too, which seem to get less welcoming the higher you go. Wincle and Wildboarclough in the foothills, rising to Dove Holes, Sparrow Pit and Nether End.

Sheffield is often held up as a case study of textbook, successful regeneration following the decimation of the steel industry and traditional manufacturing there. Perhaps Sheffield was lucky in that the loss of its staple income took place relatively quickly, prompting successive governments to shower it with vast wedges of cash. Stoke-on-Trent seemed to miss the gravy train, somehow, or at least it was made to wait for the next one, possibly because the slow, steady shrinkage of the ceramic sector didn't throw our plight into sharp enough relief.

Sheffield certainly seems to be prospering. It still has problems with employment, but according to Government statistics, forty-one per cent of workers are in category one to three jobs (managers and senior officials, professional occupations and 'associate professional and technical', whatever they are) compared to fewer than thirty per cent in Stoke-on-Trent.

A slightly higher proportion of people in the Potteries is involved in 'personal service occupations', and it's to be hoped this has little or nothing to do with the little rash of 'professional health studios' which breaks out from time to time and place to place.

In Sheffield, 21.3 per cent of workers are involved in the bottom two employment categories, but in Stoke-on-Trent the figure is 26.9 per cent, compared to a national average of 18.6 per cent. If you're interested, and so you can decide whether you are almost the lowest of the low in the eyes of official statisticians, the second from bottom band is reserved for process plant and machine operatives, which seems a bit harsh.

The lowest rung is classed as 'elementary occupations'. I don't know what this means, and, quite frankly, I can't be bothered to find out, but I imagine it would include things like drug dealers, private wheel clampers, anyone working in a large IT department ('just turn it off and turn it on again'), estate agents and professional footballers.

Average gross weekly pay for full-time workers in Sheffield was £427.40 in 2007, compared to just £382.10 in Stoke-on-Trent.

And 20 per cent of working-age people in Stoke-on-Trent have no qualifications, compared to 13.5 per cent in Sheffield – a fact almost certainly explained by the higher number of professional footballers per head of population in the Potteries.

Anyhow, shining beacon of regeneration or not, as I come off the moors, on to the ring road and get close to Hillsborough, it looks pretty much like anywhere else. I park on B&Q and walk towards the ground past the same national and international chains, in roughly the same order, as I do on the Festival Park.

I head into the stadium and, within minutes, discover that Sheffield Wednesday's ground is an architectural masterpiece of such proportions that, were he to witness it, the bloke off *Grand Designs* would experience uncontrollable seepage. When I see the tiny, wooden door with the hand-made 'Gents' sign on it, I congratulate myself on getting there before most of the three thousand other Stokies, many of whom will have bladders stretched to crisis point by fizzy lager. I open the door, and I realise I no longer have any confidence in the laws of physics or perspective or the evidence of my own eyes. I take a step back, close the door and then open it again, in the same way I imagine every first-time visitor to the Tardis must do. Facing me is the longest row of urinals I have ever seen, stretching off to the vanishing point to both my left and right.

Maybe people used to urinate more, I think, and I make a mental note to check whether it was built during the great national bladder-shrinking crisis of the early '50s.

We're right at the top of the stand, and it's a miracle the whole lot hasn't come crashing down to pitch level through the sheer weight of porcelain.

The Britannia Stadium was designed in 1996 with the aid of expensive consultants and computer programmes costing tens of thousands of pounds, but evidently Windows Turd-be-Gone Bog Design For Beginners hadn't been developed then, because I have been in crowds of twenty-seven there and still had to queue for the toilets, flies down at the ready, for the best part of ten minutes.

Hillsborough, on the other hand, was designed without software, hardware or any other sort of ware (except sanitary ware, obviously), probably by a bloke wearing a flat cap with a roll-up stuck behind his ear, and you're in, flies down, job done and out within a minute.

Being something of an expert now, I can tell you Sheffield has 23,000 people working in skilled trades occupations; and I'm willing to bet at least half of those must be plumbers and bog technicians working solely for Sheffield Wednesday, while at least 20,000 of the people in 'elementary occupations' must be on the books at Hillsborough as toilet cleaners.

Less than two days to go before the Wednesday game, within a whisker of the deadline for signing loan players riding off into the sunset without a whisper, we sign Shola Ameobi from Newcastle and Stephen Pearson from Derby.

Pearson is a midfielder who has played regularly for Derby this season, and although his club are about to take over the proud mantle of being relegated from the top flight of English football with the lowest points tally in history, he seems to have been pretty well thought of by the fans.

Ameobi appeared many times for the England under-21s, but, now twenty-six, his scoring record at club level is patchy. Since Keegan took over at Newcastle, he's only appeared twice, but he's used to playing and training with some of the best players in the world, so he's got to be worth a go. Whether he's worth the amount he will cost remains to be seen. It's widely reported this is the most expensive loan deal in history, and as well as picking up his wages of more than £20,000 a week, we're rumoured to have paid a six-figure sum for the privilege of doing so. He'd better be bloody good, I tell you. For that sort of cash, Stoke fans will expect him to score two goals a game, get the beers in after the match and come round on the Sunday to help put some shelves up.

News of the signings is met with a surge of excitement and optimism because football is different from almost every other walk of life in that change is almost always welcomed. Fans always want the manager sacked or the board sacked or the players sacked, or the whole lot of them sacked, and when it happens there is without fail a universal feeling that better days are just around the corner.

If we could just get that left-sided midfielder, we reason, or a new manager, or if that idiot of a chairman would bugger off and retire to Barbados, the good times would surely roll.

In stark contrast, though, when your boss comes up to you and tells you there may be a few changes, does your heart lift with anticipation of your life taking a turn for the better? No, it bloody doesn't; you feel slightly nauseous in the certain knowledge that within days you will be doing more hours for less money.

If your boss tells you we all need to be *receptive* to change, you know the situation will be even worse and probably involve you having to sack most of your mates.

And if your boss tells you everyone is going to have to *embrace* change, you can bet your bottom dollar he is clutching your P45 behind his back and in the process of running off with your wife.

But as football fans, we not only embrace change, we wine and dine it, get it drunk and fumble with its bra straps in a dark alley. Almost every change is viewed as positive; as a new start, a clean slate; the start of the renaissance.

Both of the new boys start today, and they look sharp and inventive – although Ameobi seems a bit too keen to beat five players in the penalty area rather than wellying the ball into the gaping net; it's no bloody wonder he's got a patchy scoring record. In fact everyone looks a whole lot better than for a long time. It's no surprise on twenty-one minutes when Cresswell cleverly diverts a cross-shot from Pearson into the net and the noise must nearly shatter 3,520 urinals a few yards away. 1-0 at half-time and it's all looking rosy.

I nip to the loos, confident I will find a space – probably with my name on it on a little brass plate polished by the category fours – and discover the Tardis has been transformed into the world's biggest smoking den. The weak electric lights and the pale afternoon coming through the frosted glass are diffused eerily through layers of fag smoke gently ebbing, flowing and rolling with the passage of people. It looks like the mist you always see in the films hanging around swamps in somewhere like Crutchscab, Louisiana, just before some fresh-faced, out-of-state lovers get unspeakable things done to them by a group of slack-jawed, spittle-lipped inbred locals who then hack them into untidy steaks and cook them Cajun style. I look around uneasily for the spooky bloke from the monumental masons, but I can't see him.

The strata of smoke are all beautifully co-ordinated yet very clearly defined shades of grey from almost white to almost black, and I wonder whether each one represents a different brand of cigarette. Maybe that band of gunmetal grey there is a Benson's, while that ominous oily black slick sneaking around at ankle level is Albanian Lungscraper rolling tobacco bought off the bloke down the pub. (I don't know if it's just me, but as an ex-smoker I find myself still obsessed with everything to do with the habit. It's testament to the addictive power of nicotine that I probably think about smoking every third minute. What with men thinking about sex every seventeen seconds or whatever it's meant to be, that doesn't leave me with a lot of time to concentrate on anything else, which probably explains a lot. Like why I throw teaspoons into the bin after I've dried them up; or why, when asked what I would like with my burger I often reply: 'Twenty Marlboro Lights and a shag, please.' Actually, I'm pretty sure I've never said it out loud, but I couldn't guarantee it.) Anyhow, I consider studying the smoke formations in the miraculous Sheffield Wednesday toilets, asking people what sort of fags they're smoking, making notes and perhaps taking pictures, but decide against it after taking into consideration potential long-term health problems caused by passive inhalation and the risk of unpleasant splashback incidents.

In any case, the smokers are getting a bit militant.

'One of us smoking, there's only one of us smoking, one of us smoooooking, there's only one of us smoooooking,' a bloke next to me starts singing.

'Two of us smoking, there's only two of us smoking ... ,' joins in another down the line.

Within seconds it's up to twenty-three and more and more people are lighting up ostentatiously. I can't make out who this uprising is aimed at. The Government for introducing the smoking ban? The stewards in the ground who have no intention of getting involved? Non-smokers? Whichever, I head back towards my seat. As the bog door opens and closes, it releases a billow of cigarette fumes which rolls down the concourse like someone's running a hippy workshop on Native American smoke signals.

The first ten minutes of the second half are all Stoke, but then someone presses the 'snatch defeat from the jaws of victory' button and we collapse. Panic ensues and the Stoke fans wait for the inevitable.

A little guy in gold boots called Songo'o (the little guy's called Songo'o, I mean, not the boots. Songo'o would be a stupid name for boots) is tearing us apart every time he gets the ball. Sure enough, in the eighty-third minute, our confidence already gone for its early bath, changed, finished post-match interviews and into its second table dance, we back off him five, ten, fifteen yards, just begging him to shoot and put us out of our misery. He obliges, of course, and we spend the next ten minutes clinging on desperately for a point.

But you know what? I'm still fairly happy. In fact, I'm bloody delirious. Once again, the teams around us towards the top of the table are doing even more than we are to shoot themselves in the foot – it's like we've all got the footballing equivalent of a self-harming problem. As the final whistle goes, the buzz goes around that West Brom have lost 3-2 and Bristol have drawn 1-1. Strangers raise their eyebrows at each other and give knowing smiles of relief as it dawns on us that not only are we still top, but we've also put a fraction more distance between us and West Brom with games rapidly running out.

As we shuffle down the stands towards the exit, the public address announcer is reading out final scores.

'Colchester three, West Bromwich Albion three,' he says. Shit, they must have got a late, late equaliser. Oh well, at least we're still top.

'Correction. Colchester three, West Bromwich Albion four.'

For fuck's sake, you are *joking*. Oh well, at least we're still top.

As I'm walking back to the car I find out Bristol scored in injury time to beat Norwich 2-1. We're down to second.

I drive back through torrential rain over hills that are as dark and bleak as my mood.

To: BBC

Dear Sir or Madam,

Just a quick note to say thank you for your truly groundbreaking new series *I'd Do Anything*. A show based on getting the audience to spend money voting for desperate karaoke singers? Genius. I can't think where the idea came from.

Enriching and innovative as *I'd Do Anything* is, however, could I suggest a couple of improvements?

Firstly, I think it should be on more often and

for many more weeks. I don't know how long *I'd Do Anything* is going to run for, but it can't be sufficient.

It seemed to me all those other unique, innovative programmes that have been exactly the same as this (*Strictly Come Dancing* series one to 283, that Maria one, *Any Dream Will Do*, that really awful cheap one with the tribute acts, *Celebrity Pets On Ice* and *Pregnant Nuns On Acid*, to name but a fraction) were only on twice a day, six days a week, fifty-four weeks a year. This is obviously nowhere near enough.

Actually, scrub *Pregnant Nuns On Acid*. If memory serves, that was a Channel 5 documentary.

And secondly, I really think the dramatic pause before you reveal who has got the least number of votes and is going home needs to be extended. I'm talking about that bit just after the presenter says: 'I can now reveal, the mediocre amateur going home this week is ... ' You know, the synthesized bommmmmmmmmmmmmmm, that goes on until the poor saps who have spent most of their pensions voting for these clowns think their tellys are broken. It could stand being a good fifteen seconds longer. At the moment, I barely have time to scream: 'AAAAAGGGGGGGGGGHHHHHHHH! Switch off this lazy, greedy, depressing, TV-by-formula before I smash the set, storm out of the house, go on an indiscriminate killing spree and then turn the gun on myself!' before the bommm's over and I know I might, at least this week, survive the brain-sapping crap being beamed into my living room day after day.

And no, I can't turn it off. My wife would do her biscuit. And no, I'm not going to leave the room while it's on (except maybe to fetch the shells for the shotgun). Why should I let London marketing twonks in trendy glasses – twonks who have undoubtedly been possessed by Satan as part of his dastardly plot to turn the brains of perfectly decent folk into pork pie jelly – force me out of my own bloody living room?

Many thanks for your time,

David Johnson

CHAPTER 22

Five games to go. We're not playing until Monday because the game's on telly. Hull aren't playing this weekend, and today West Brom are playing in the semi-final of the FA Cup, so at least we can't drop any further down the table.

As a kid, I used to love the FA Cup. The final was always on the BBC, and maybe I'm remembering this through rose-tinted spectacles, but the coverage seemed to start at about nine in the morning, and it always featured The Road To Wembley – the round-by-round account of how the finalists had made it through to the big day.

Then they would always manage to find a family split down the middle by footballing allegiance and the house would be decked out half in red and half in blue, or whatever the colours happened to be that year.

There would be cameras at the hotels where each team was staying, and as they left for the stadium, a steady procession of perms, mullets and moustaches would duck out of the hotel entrance, perhaps give a smile to the camera, and trot up the stairs onto the team coach.

The film would cut to Wembley Way, and the seemingly unending, unstoppable march of people and flags never failed to give me goosebumps. By the time my dad came in at about quarter to three, I'd be in a lather of excitement.

Perceptions change, of course, as do priorities, but I still enjoy watching the latter stages of the competition, so I'm looking forward to the West Brom v Portsmouth semi-final later on.

'But you've got to paint the soffits.'

I explain I have reached the age of forty-one without having the faintest idea of what a soffit is, and I have absolutely no desire to bridge that gap in my knowledge – let alone actually paint one of these mysterious things.

Thirty-five minutes later I'm up a ladder. It starts to hail.

The next day – the Sunday – I climb the ladders to apply the final coat of paint to the soffits (if you don't know what they are, look it up – it's too much effort to explain and I'm trying to blot out the whole sorry episode from my memory) as the Cardiff v Barnsley semi-final kicks off. It starts to snow. Heavily.

Monday comes around, and the edgy feeling I have all day at work is lifted only briefly when we discover a coffee stain in the exact shape of a horse's head on the tray. I just can't quite get this foolish optimism and sense of fate back in the bottle. If we win tonight against Crystal Palace, we would go two points clear at the top of the table. Okay, other teams will have games in hand over us, but I'd much rather have the points in the bag.

We hear the bad news as we're driving to the game. Liam Lawrence has been injured. Lawrence has undoubtedly been our most effective player all season, scoring fourteen goals from midfield and creating a hatful more – in fact he has been one of the best players in the whole league, and one of the only members of our team who is regularly picked out by the national media as being able to do more than toe-punt the ball towards some distant, bumbling centre forward.

Not only that, Pulis decides not to play Ricardo Fuller, who is available again after being suspended for a couple of weeks, with new-boy Ameobi. The fans are desperate to see it – two talented strikers who like the ball at their feet and can make things happen in the blink of an eye. Instead, he opts to play Ameobi with Sidibe. The same Sidibe who has, in fairness, run his gangly legs off all season, but who has only scored two goals. I know *keepers* who have scored more goals in a season.

Only 15,700 turn up, partly because the game's on the telly, but also because the support has been so fragile this season, without the belief to see it over the rocky patches, and without the promise of exciting football by way of compensation if we lose. The atmosphere is a mixture of tension and sullen resignation, and it's no surprise Palace come out and rip us apart.

They are quick and precise and imaginative and they run rings round us. They've got Scott Sinclair on loan from Chelsea and he's good enough to carry off the show-off gold boots he's wearing.

We're 2-0 down at half-time and, although we batter them in the second half and get a goal back, we never look like taking a point, let alone the three that we really need. It doesn't help that Palace waste time from the second they score the first goal in such a brazen fashion it's almost admirable. A succession of players go down with injuries that, judging by the poor, writhing, screaming victims, must have been caused by automatic gunfire from the stands, followed by the contraction of rabies a fraction ahead of being trampled on by a herd of bison. Fuller comes on after an hour and does enough to convince pretty much everyone he should have been on from the start, and then Jay Bothroyd, who we've taken on loan from Wolves, comes on in his own gold boots but, next to Sinclair, he looks like one of the ugly sisters hobbling about in the wrong-sized slipper.

'Thank God for that,' says Andy as we trudge towards Cardiac Hill. 'At least we'll still be able to get a parking space next season.'

Back in the car, Tony Pulis tells us Fuller was left out because he was a bit stale after not playing for a couple of weeks and the manager wanted forty minutes out of him.

'We were hoping we would be well in the game by the time we brought Ric on, but unfortunately it didn't go for us.'

Good thinking, Tony; without doubt the best way to make sure you are 'well in the game' is to leave your best players on the bench.

'I really had to talk Ric into playing, which he was obviously desperate to do,' says Tony, making absolutely no sense whatsoever.

The upshot is that if the other teams win their games in hand we will be fourth – finally, after being given chance after chance to pull away, we have let it slip from our fingers.

To: Lancôme UK
Dear Sir/Madam,
I had the good fortune the other night to see an advert for one of your products which has been developed with the laudable aim of elongating the appearance of eyelashes. (Please pass on my apologies to your advertising agency, I can't for the life of me remember what this mascara was called, in spite of the colossal amount of Lancôme's money they must have spent.)

There was a series of profile shots of rather strange-looking women whose eyelashes were so long it must be a constant battle to keep scabby-kneed children from tying rope swings to them.

At one point in the advert I saw the words 'Lash inserts used' flash briefly at the bottom of the screen, and I would be grateful if you could help me settle a bet. My wife tells me this means you used false eyelashes to show how effective your product is. I'm ashamed to say I laughed in her face and told her she was either drunk or stupid.

I explained that was impossible. That would be like an advert showing a second-hand Mini Metro leaving a Porsche in its wake and the message 'Actual engine used is from a Ferrari' appearing for slightly less than a second at the bottom. Or a commercial featuring a group of oh-so-cool friends laughing, dancing and high-fiving each other on the beach as they take orgasmic slugs from their bottles of imported lager being run with the caveat: 'Actual beer will taste like tramp urine, make your hair and teeth fall out and lead to addiction. You will die alone and destitute in a council house crack den.'

I mean, if that sort of thing was allowed, where the hell would it stop? Fast food chains using photographs of dishes bearing no resemblance to the slop they actually sell? Estate agents describing houses as 'convenient for transport links', when what they actually mean is 'on the central reservation of the M6'? It'd be bloody anarchy, that's what it'd be. Please confirm my wife is delusional – I'll split the tenner with you.

Regards,

David Johnson

CHAPTER 23

I'm writing this on Tuesday, the night after the Crystal Palace game. West Brom are playing after their narrow defeat in the FA cup semi-final. After eighty minutes they are losing 1-0. They win 2-1 and go top, sending us down to third, out of the automatic promotion places, the £60 million glory seats, and sliding back into obscurity where everyone – including me on occasions – seems to think we belong.

Now it's Wednesday, and tonight Watford are playing their game in hand at home to Barnsley, who are third from bottom. Watford are a point behind us, and if they win they go top and we go fourth, free-falling to failure. We have won just once in our last eight games, but our captain Andy Griffin says in *The Sentinel* today he thinks we'll go up automatically; and I don't want to believe him – I really don't – but I can't help myself. Why shouldn't we do it?

Apart from Hull, who have done some sort of deal with the Devil to turn themselves into Real Madrid, and Colin Wanker's bunch of conmen, all of us in the top six are just a bit rubbish.

It speaks volumes that Bristol City, who have been at or near the top for the entire season, have scored a pathetic forty-nine goals so far. Colchester, who are at the bottom and doomed to relegation, have scored fifty-seven.

Sure enough, Watford collapse spectacularly and lose 3-0.

Four games to go, and it's just getting too tense. Every game we play becomes the most important in more than a decade and I'm as obsessed with the results of other teams as I am with our own.

Today it's Coventry away. Lawrence is still injured , but Pulis includes him as a substitute and the fans are going to get their wish to see Fuller and Ameobi playing together – now we'll see some football.

Before the game, Pulis sets up a huge screen in the away team dressing room and the players watch Al Pacino's inspirational speech from *Any Given Sunday*.

It starts: 'I don't know what to say, really. Three minutes to the biggest battle of our professional lives comes down to today. Either we heal as a team or we are going to crumble. Inch by inch, play by play till we're finished.'

He talks about fighting back into the light and tells them he's too old to do it for them and so screwed up he can't stand the face he sees in the mirror. Life is just a game of inches, he says, and all of them have to be willing to sweat blood for every inch on the pitch.

'I'll tell you this: in any fight it is the guy who is willing to die who is going to win that inch. And I know if I am going to have any life anymore, it is because I am still willing to fight and die for that inch because that is what living is. The six inches in front of your face.'

He calls for sacrifice and urges everyone to look into his neighbour's eyes and see the willingness to die for the people around you.

He finishes: 'That's a team, gentlemen, and either we heal now, as a team, or we will die as individuals. That's football, guys.

'Now. Whattaya gonna do?'

Yes, it's about American football, but who could fail to be inspired by it? Just thinking about it again fills me with the urge to grab the nearest person by the lapels and scream: 'GO OOOOOOOOOOOOOOOOOOON STOKE!' into his face from two inches. Who could flinch from looking squarely into his neighbour's eyes in the certain knowledge that dying for the team is infinitely preferable to failure as individuals? Who could fail to feel his back straighten, his chest swell, his jaw set, his balls grow and his testosterone flow?

The bloody Stoke players, of course, that's who. I'm listening on the radio in our half-built kitchen, and, by all accounts, we go out and play our worst forty-five minutes of football of the season. Coventry, who are in danger of being relegated, are all over us. We have no imagination, no movement, no chances and we're trying to play defensive football with a defence which has forgotten how to defend.

After twenty-five minutes, Ameobi has to go off with a hamstring injury, and he's replaced by the less-than-prolific Sidibe. Five minutes after that, Coventry get a penalty, go 1-0 up and it sounds as if they will go on to get a hatful. Fifteen minutes later, skipper Andy Griffin pulls a hamstring too, and he's replaced by Shawcross. No-one seems to know how we make it to half-time without being three or four-nil down.

Now, I don't know what Tony Pulis said to the players during the break, but it certainly knocked that wimp Al Pacino into a cocked hat. My guess is something like: 'I don't know what to say, really. Ten minutes to the biggest battle of our professional lives.

'Now I can't do it for you. I'm too old. I made every wrong choice a middle-aged man could make. I decided to manage Stoke for a start, and what a bloody thankless task that is, I can tell you. And lately I can't even stand the face I see in the mirror. Oh, hang on, that's Jon. Stop lurking behind me, Parkin and go and sit down. And you've got ketchup all down your shirt.

'Life is just a game of inches. Stop sniggering, lads, I'm trying to be serious.

'I know if I am going to have any life any more, it is because I am still willing to fight and die for that inch, because that is what living is. The six inches in front of your face. Oh, come on guys, cut it out – how old are you?

'Oh, and did I mention Mr Coates is willing to double your win bonus?'

I don't really mean that. Talking to people who went to the game, every player looked as if they really *were* prepared to die to win an inch for the team and they really *were* willing to fight for the six inches in front of their face rather than the six zeros in their bank balances.

Even before we get a penalty, the noise being generated by the three thousand-plus Stokies is just incredible. Fuller scores the spot-kick, and from then on it's one-way traffic.

It's been obvious over the past few weeks how much we've missed Liam Lawrence (he and Fuller have scored thirty goals between them so far this season), and with twenty-five minutes to go, Pulis takes the gamble and brings him on. The noise cranks up to a constant, frenzied, primeval cry for blood, and with just over ten minutes to go it happens. Cresswell bears down for a one-on-one with the keeper, but he overruns it and from the resulting collision the ball rebounds to Lawrence just outside the area. He hits it on the volley, past desperately retreating defenders, and into the back of the net.

One of Alison's friends has come round to see our bombsite of a kitchen, and she looks on in alarm as I run back and forth across the room in silence, too full of joy to make a sound. I sprint up and down on the spot pumping my arms and, slowly at first, I find my voice: 'aaaaaaaaaaaAAAAAAAAAAAAGGGGGHHHH GET INNNNNNN!'

You know we're going to hang on, it's just one of those sort of days, and the unconvincing performances and poor results of the last couple of months have been forgotten.

Crystal Palace have won, and I wouldn't put it past Colin Wanker's boys to make a late charge for promotion, but Bristol draw and Hull draw. Half an hour after we beat Coventry,

West Brom kick off against Watford, and a draw in this game would be a gift from the gods for us and a setback for both of our rivals.

It ends 1-1, and we're top of the table by one point with three games to go.

On the Monday at work I read interviews with our players and they all sound bullish and confident and they put forward solid arguments as to why Stoke will be going up. I feel myself swelling with confidence. Then I go on the internet and read the interviews with players from Hull, West Brom and Bristol City, and they are just as bullish and put forward just as good cases for their teams' chances. I'm in a froth of uncertainty again. On Tuesday I keep sneaking greedy, furtive glances at the table in the paper, like a vicar with a pornographic playing card in his pocket, and every time I get that little jolt of shock and pleasure to see us at the top. I read our players' bullish interviews again and I just know we're going up. I can smell it.

That night, West Brom and Hull play their games in hand. West Brom beat Wolves in one of the games I had hoped would put a spanner in the works for the Baggies and Hull beat Barnsley. It couldn't be worse. We're now third in the table and out of the automatic promotion places. We're doomed to another season in this awful division, I just know we are. I can smell it.

CHAPTER 24

Three games to go. For the first time in my life football is having a real impact on my daily routine. I can't concentrate on anything for more than a few moments and I frequently come to with a start, my screen jumping back into focus and I realise I have spent the last seven minutes worrying about Liam Lawrence's groin strain.

Typically, I work with both a West Brom fan and a Hull fan. If both clubs are promoted, the pain of watching my colleagues' joy, overhearing them talking excitedly to their mates on the phone, will be just too much. I will almost certainly have to kill them.

The potential for humiliation is too great, but it's obvious they are going through the same turmoil as me. I may be thinking about some bloke's groin, but they are stewing over similar uncertainties, working out the same set of permutations and predicting the outcome of the same games and we've all developed the same exaggeratedly casual mouse technique for covering up football websites as the boss approaches.

So this is it then. Arguably the biggest game in the club's history. If we don't beat Bristol today we can forget going up automatically. Incredibly, after a run with just two wins in nine games, we're still within spitting distance of the Premier League. But we're running out of games, and we won't be given any more chances. West Brom have come good again and are top with seventy-four points. Hull and us are on seventy-two, but we're third on goal difference. Bristol are one point behind us, Watford are fifth, and Crystal Palace have surged up the table and are now in the last play-off place.

Andy gets the train in from Manchester (conversation with the woman selling tickets on board: 'Do you want a single or return?'

'What's the difference?'

'One gets you there and the other gets you there and back.'

'That's not exactly what I meant.') and we go for a few beers before the game.

Andy's decided he has once again found his love for the game after Higginbotham's transfer to Sunderland all but destroyed his faith. In Andy's eyes, we rescued a player from the obscurity of reserve football, gave him the chance to shine and as soon as he gets the chance for a big money move, he's off like a whippet.

I'm not sure. Sometimes I think we expect too much of players who are paid mind-boggling sums of money a few years after ditching the school uniform. I'm pretty confident that if I had been burdened with the same pressures and beckoned by the same temptations at that age I would have made a monumental arse-up of it and been exposed in the tabloids with some fuzzy mobile phone shot of me snorting cocaine from a prostitute's bum cheeks.

In any event Andy is once again, as he describes it, 'feeling the love', his belief restored by a team which may not be particularly good, and which on occasions has been truly awful, but which all season has never looked anything other than committed to the cause. But it is critical for us that Liam Lawrence, rated as the best in the Championship by those statistics companies which analyse every pass, interception, shot, foul, tackle and bowel movement of every player, is fit for the rest of the season. Pulis has been saying all week it's touch and go whether Lawrence will be fit, but I've got a sneaking suspicion he's just been playing mind games with Bristol.

Kick-off is at 5.20 p.m. because the game's on Sky, which means we will know the results of the other matches before the Stoke game starts. We're standing by the bar when a shout goes up and the big screen on the wall shows Sheffield United have gone ahead against Hull. We text a mate who's a United fan, but he tells us not to get giddy because they've had a man sent off and it's only just half-time. A short while later and the bar erupts again: 2-0, and that's the way it stays.

West Brom win, and we can pretty much forget them now; they'll go up as champions. So it's all about second place, and Watford lose 2-0 at home to Crystal Palace. It could hardly be better. If we win today, promotion is there for the taking.

Although the game is being televised, 24,500 people are in the ground, the biggest crowd at the Britannia Stadium for five years and the mood is buoyant after we find out Lawrence is playing. When him and Fuller are both fit we look a different team. According to the statisticians, Fuller is in the top five strikers in the division according to the statisticians. Big Mama, our other striker, has worked his arse off all season and contributed much more than many people give him credit for, but he's only scored two goals, and unsurprisingly he hasn't troubled the top one hundred list all season.

As soon as we kick off, it's obvious Lawrence is either completely fit and Pulis has been having us all on, or he has been force-fed amphetamines and steroids for three days. He's superb, everyone seems to be playing at or close to the top of his game and the atmosphere is everything it usually isn't – intimidating, loud and constant.

We're all over them, and within fifteen minutes, Lawrence sends over a great free kick and Big Mama leaps like a great Malian salmon to bury an unstoppable header into the net.

160

I know they probably don't have salmon in Mali, and if they do, they're probably not six foot four and black, but you get my drift and I've got no intention of trawling through the internet to find maps showing the distribution of gamefish in western Africa.

The relief and joy is uncontainable. As I do circles on the spot with my arms in the air, hundreds of people in my sightline are throwing themselves around uncontrollably, hugging their neighbours and hurling meaningless screams of triumph at no-one in particular.

Under normal circumstances, we would now be in for seventy minutes of hell as the players sit back too deep and hack at anything that comes near them as the opponents lay siege to our goal. But nothing changes from the restart; we're calm and confident and Bristol have got nothing to offer. Before long, Sidibe flicks on to Fuller on the halfway line, spins to receive the immediate return pass and charges thirty yards for a one-on-one with the goalkeeper.

I suppose I must have seen Mama score one of these in the three years he's been with us, but I'm buggered if I can remember it. It's on his right foot, and Mama favours his left to such an extent I'm surprised he doesn't walk in circles, and he's got far too much time to think. But he slides it under the advancing keeper with the confidence of someone slotting home his thirty-fifth of the season and I suspect he's had his head in the same bucket of amphetamines as Lawrence.

We're completely in control and enjoying the party until Bristol get one back on sixty-seven minutes.

We go into complete meltdown and the last ten minutes are just awful. They run us ragged, but when Shawcross somehow manages to clear what looks like a certain goal off the line, you get the feeling we're going to do it.

And so it turns out. It's been a deserved win and a performance that, in the main, showed a side rapidly regaining form and confidence at exactly the right time.

We're second behind West Brom and three points ahead of Hull. Next week, if Hull lose to Crystal Palace – who look as unstoppable as Hull themselves did a couple of weeks ago – and we beat Colchester we're up with a game to spare.

CHAPTER 25

Does any of this really matter? I don't know, but it does to me, and it feels like it's important in some broader, cosmic sense. All over the world, people worship different gods, eat different food, talk different languages, laugh at different jokes, enjoy the fruits of their wealth or find their meals on the rubbish dump, huddle themselves against the cold or sweat in the heat, look out of their windows at trees and fields or tower blocks or jungle or desert or sea. But we all need to see the underdog win occasionally, we all need to witness the meek inheriting a tiny speck of the earth for once, we all need to know that the kid with the glasses and the spots and the stutter can get the girl once in a while and we all need to know people like us can occasionally – just occasionally – have dreams come true.

This is our dreamtime, but if we do it – if we, please God, manage to stumble over the finishing line without some monumental fuck-up – we will be doing it to stuff it up every single person who has taken the piss out of us this season and we'll be doing it for silent, browbeaten underdogs the world over.

It's also important to us as a club. Earlier this season our chief executive said Stoke City were the worst-supported side in the Championship if you analyse the proportion of the population in the catchment area which actually goes to games. Part of this is probably down to the low wages in the area, but not all of it. Some of it has got to be the result of a twenty-three-year absence from the top division, and the lack of entertainment served up by many of the eighteen managers and caretaker managers and hundreds of players we have had since then.

Tony Pulis could never be accused of dishing up scintillating football, but he recognises the importance of this season to both the club and the city. He knows we have a lost generation of fans, lured away from their local team by the bright lights of the satellite channels and the chance for instant gratification supporting one of the Premier League big boys with their slick merchandising and their one-track marketing departments bent on delivering 'added value', or whatever the latest hideous corporate phrase is, to their owners or shareholders.

It's taken until the second-to-last game of the season, but the fans are united behind a team which has shown guts and determination all season and a manager who has taken this club – this founder of the Football League with its lost generation of fans drifting rootless to Man United or Arsenal or Chelsea – to the brink of the big time.

Colchester's ground holds only 6,300 people, so maybe it's no surprise they're planning a move to an out-of-town site after 101 years, but it still seems a shame. Fifteen years or so after the first clubs upped sticks from the back yards of their audience to reappear in stadia which look like spaceships just come to land by chance on soulless retail parks, it's obvious the trend hasn't been an unqualified success; but I can understand the reasons for it, and the influx of raucous fans and the congestion that goes with it can make for an uneasy relationship between a traditional town centre club and the community around it.

Having said that, what sort of problems could a maximum of 6,300 people cause? There are villages in the highlands of Scotland with bigger populations. Whatever, Stoke's visit is the last ever game to be played at Layer Road, and I can't help thinking that's going to count against us. Colchester have already been relegated and last week they got battered 5-1 by Coventry, but I'm afraid they will rise to the occasion, while we will freeze at the last moment as the implications of the game for both teams hit home. I ask myself if the current crop of Colchester players, many of whom may have little or no genuine connection to the community they represent, should know – or care – that the first game to be played at Layer Road was in 1907 between the 4th Battalion King's Rifle and South Weald. Can they really be expected to feel any resonance from 1909 when the King's Rifle were sent overseas to India and Colchester Town took over the ground? Do they even know about Colchester's famous victory over the mighty Leeds United in the FA Cup in 1971? Probably not, I reassure myself, but they will certainly feel the atmosphere charged with the mixed emotions of fans, some of whom have been coming here for fifty or sixty years.

What's more, Teddy Sheringham, the oldest professional player in England and one of the most prolific strikers of the modern era, came to rest here after he realised his aching bones couldn't cut it in the Premier League any more.

So the script is written for Colchester to win a pulsating final game at Layer Road, probably 3-2, with Sheringham coming on as substitute to score the winner two minutes into injury time.

In spite of all this, I've felt less nervous since the victory over Bristol, and I've been able to at least partially concentrate at work, narrowly heading off disciplinary action. Now it's the morning of Saturday, 26 April, the sun is shining and as I sit outside Tesco feeding 50p pieces into the Bob The Builder ride (for Harry, you understand, not me) I can feel the first genuine warmth of spring on my face. The optimism is rising, and I make an effort to remember everything I do that morning – shopping, watching my nephew play football, playing with Harry on the slide – to provide some sort of everyday framework for my memories of what could be one of the greatest achievements in my club's history and one of the greatest days of my life.

Stoke have only been given nine hundred tickets for the game, so the club has organised a beamback at the Britannia Stadium. Last year a similar event was put on for the last game of the season, away at Queens Park Rangers, which could have seen us make it into the play-offs. Back then, we all called it the big screen.

'Are you going to watch it on the big screen?'

'Yeah, let's have a couple of beers in town and watch it on the big screen.'

This season, though, realising fans are prepared to pay £12 a pop, the marketing department has got involved and we've all been duped into calling it the 'beamback', which sounds as if Captain Kirk will be twiddling the knobs behind the scenes.

'Hey, are you going to the beamback?'

'Yeah, let's have a couple of beers in town and then go to the beamback.'

'Affirmative, Captain.'

It turns out it's pretty much the same as last year, though – a big screen which becomes smaller and smaller as we climb to our seats, and a couple of technicians wandering around trying to synch the radio commentary with the pictures.

But, other than Colchester, I wouldn't be anywhere else, and neither would the other eight thousand fans here – considerably more people than are in the whole of Layer Road – and that's why, collectively, we've shelled out close to £800,000 to watch an oversized telly.

We just need to be with other fans today. Which is why my sister has come up with Neil and CJ from their home near St Albans, about seventy miles from Colchester. They couldn't get tickets for the game either, so they're making the two hundred and eighty-mile round trip to the Potteries, lured by the irresistible magnetic attraction of people with the same dreams and insecurities as yourself.

I briefly wonder whether the dickhead who sat behind me at the Scunthorpe game has felt the same pull, or those countless others who have found any number of excuses for not coming to the games.

Pulis is right to talk about a lost generation of fans. Just over eleven thousand people came to watch us beat QPR 3-1 at the back end of November and two weeks before only twelve thousand turned up for the Sheffield United game. But since February the feeling that something special is going on here has seeped through the streets, fields, pubs and workplaces of North Staffordshire and South Cheshire. Almost twenty-one thousand were at the Scunthorpe game, 23,500 came to see us play Ipswich, twenty thousand were at the Blackpool game and last week 24,500 came to watch the Bristol City game – a match which people could have watched on the telly at home or in the pub. The last game of the season, next Sunday at home to Leicester, has already been sold out for a week.

Before the game begins, the public address system plays Pottermouth's Battle Cry, and, although you can only make out one word in ten because of the interference, it still brings a lump to the throat. We more or less know it off by heart now anyway, and the rise and fall of the poem against the strains of *The Planets Suite* by Holst stirs the emotions in us all.

God knows why, really. It started as a spoof in a comedy voice left anonymously on Radio Stoke's answering machine before appearing on the internet set to a slideshow of Stoke-on-Trent landmarks, Stoke fans, old Stoke players and a duck. National radio picked it up, then the national papers, and within twenty-four hours of being posted on YouTube it had received ten thousand hits. The last time I looked more than sixty thousand people had viewed one of the several versions on the site.

It first surfaced just after we'd lost at home to Palace earlier this month, when so many of us were heading back into a pit of despair and uncertainty. In a daft sort of way it helped, lifting the spirit just when it was needed most.

Since then, mick-take or not, it has captured the mood perfectly and been a real factor in building unity and momentum towards the end of this emotionally bruising campaign. It might not be Shakespeare, but, I kid you not, teachers at some of the city's high schools are using it to help kids relate to poetry and to encourage them to express their feelings through words other than 'no', 'yeah' and 'dunno'.

People leave messages on several of the sites featuring the Battle Cry talking about the impact the poem has had on them, including one curiously moving one written completely in text message shorthand by a youngster who cried during his geography lesson when the teacher read it out to the class.

Parts of it may not mean a huge amount if you're not from North Staffordshire or South Cheshire or a Stoke fan, with its references to local landmarks, obscure retailers, old local radio presenters, long-extinct public transport companies and contributors to phone-ins, but you'll get a flavour and I think it's worth recording here because it was so prevalent and it never failed to raise a smile when you heard it driving to work or on the way to the game.

This is a call to the men who wear the red and white
A heartfelt battle cry
As you enter the crucial fight
A final inspiration to lead you into war
A chance to remind you of what you're fighting for

'Cause as you reach for the Premiership
As you sweat blood and tears
You carry us all on your backs
All our hopes and fears

So do it for the Potteries
Do it for all of us
Do it for Josiah Wedgwood, and for a PMT bus

Do it for Nigel Johnson, do it for Sir Stan
Do it for singing toddlers and for my old man

Do it for Trentham Gardens
Do it for Mow Cop
Do it for Pat McGarry and his paper shop

Do it for Wrights Pies
Do it for oatcakes
Take us to the Prem whatever it takes

Do it for the blokes as call each other duck
Do it for Andy in his dumper truck
Do it for the man who shouts 'SENTINEL!'
Do it for Lime Kiln Bank
Do it for Nick Hancock
Do it for Sam Plank

Do it for the Boothen End and its deafening sound
Do it for Denis Smith and the old Victoria Ground
Do it for Alan Hudson
Do it for Gordon Banks
Do it for the glory and our eternal thanks

Do it for the Meir tunnel
For Slash – *Sweet Child o' Mine*

Do it for Royal Doulton
Do it for the old mines

Do it for going up 'anley duck
Do it for Mark Stein
For Waddo, for Ritchie and Ian in Scholar Green

Do it for Longton bus station
For the shirt on yer back
Do it for Owd Grandad Piggott
And for Club-paper Jack
And we'll be with you, every step along the way
Down the Brit, United and Arsenal, every week on
Match Of The Day

Do it for the Stokies around the world near and far
Do it, do it, Pulis, please do it
Owrayt? Ta-ra!

So as the beamback beams back and the nine hundred Stoke fans partying in the Essex sun flicker into life on the screen across the other side of an empty pitch, we know if we win today and Hull lose or draw against Crystal Palace that's it; we're up, twenty-three years of hurt over; erased, eradicated and forgotten in ninety glorious minutes.

About 899 of the Stokies at Colchester are in replica tops of one vintage or another, and the white stripes gleam in the sun. During the warm-up, Liam Lawrence has to avoid some re-enactment enthusiast dressed as a soldier from the Civil War, then the ball is brought on by the Lord Mayor accompanied by a bagpiper.

All the pomp reminds me what this game means to Colchester. For us, it's certainly the most important game since our solitary major trophy triumph in the League Cup in 1972, but this is one of the most momentous days for the U's in more than a century, and my optimism is soon swamped by a horrible nagging dread; the same feeling of low-level, permanent sickness you get when you know you've done something wrong and it's only a matter of time before you're found out.

To start with, the atmosphere at the Britannia is flat. Self-consciously, some groups try to get the singing going, but the tension and the slightly surreal feeling that eight thousand people are all in the world's biggest living room watching the television is hard to overcome.

We're having all the possession, all the chances and corner after corner, but we just can't get the bloody thing in the net. Or anywhere near it for that matter. But, unlike on match days, people are allowed to bring beer to their seats, and rapidly-receding inhibitions allow the noise level to crank up. Eight thousand people stand up, cheer and chant at eleven players two hundred miles away.

But after twenty minutes the news comes through the radio on Ash's mobile that Hull have gone one up. The despondency spreads like a slick, and the importance of winning this game rears into focus, above the small big screen, above the stands and blotting out the blue sky until it's all I can see.

Until about twenty minutes later, when the radio commentary from Colchester is the first to tell us Palace have equalised. Belief pours through us again, and we scream the players on, completely oblivious to the miles between us. In injury time of the first half, Richard Cresswell has a header well saved by the keeper, but the ball spills out to Lawrence, who stubs it back towards goal; it hits Cresswell's knee and somehow squeezes over the line. All hell breaks loose.

We don't play well in the second half, but I don't care – none of us does. We're going up to the Premier League; not next year or sometime or next week, but today, in forty-five minutes, in thirty minutes, in ten minutes, in five minutes.

Five minutes from time we hear Hull have scored, and the heads sinking into hands on the screen are mirrored ten times over at the Britannia. We're not going up today.

Seconds later, still trying to come to terms with the Hull score, Colchester's Clive Platt loops a header which seems to take three weeks to sail over a clutch of players, over Carlo Nash and to drop into the back of the net. Instantly, without having to formulate the thoughts, I know we've thrown it all away again; that by the end of next week West Brom and Hull will be promoted and we will be destined for failure in the play-offs.

But wait. There's confusion. Why aren't the Colchester players celebrating? Why are some of the Stoke fans over there punching the air? The goal has been disallowed for a push, and I collapse into my seat.

When the final whistle goes and Hull's win is confirmed, it feels as if we've lost. We were so close for so long. On the drive home, though, I manage to regain my perspective. We've come through a tricky game with a win, the players as always looked determined and focused, we're top of the table with one game to go and no matter what anyone else does we only need a draw against Leicester.

It's all set up for a day like no other next Sunday. Almost twenty-eight thousand fans will be at the Britannia Stadium, we're playing a team who are fourth from bottom and we just need to avoid losing to be promoted to the most watched league in the world. What could possibly go wrong?

Monday. We're tidying the kitchen, but I keep bobbing into the front room to check the West Brom score on the television, and for the life of me I can't work out what result would be best for us. If they lose, it means they are right back in the mire and they will be one of three teams, along with us and Hull, fighting for two automatic promotion spots. If they win, they have done it and there will be two teams fighting for one place, so weighing up the probabilities I want West Brom to lose. But they're playing Southampton, who, like Leicester, are desperate to avoid relegation. If Southampton win, it will make it more likely that on Sunday, Leicester are going to have to throw everything at us in a last-ditch bid for survival, so from that point of view I want Southampton to lose. So would a draw be the best result or the worst result for us? Before I can make a decision, I realise Alison is saying something to me.

'You can't put both chopping boards into the dishwasher this early in the week.'

'I'm sorry?'

'I said you can't put both chopping boards in the dishwasher this early in the week.'

'Why not? What difference does it make whether it's Monday or ... oh, for ... never mind, I really haven't got the room in my head to think about this at the moment.'

By the time I decide a draw is probably the worst result for us, the game's over and it's a draw. Unless Hull win their last game of the season 12-0 – and unless they are allowed to carry guns this is highly unlikely – then West Brom are up. I watch the celebrations at the Hawthorns and I realise how badly I want to be a part of it.

Tuesday. 'What do you think about these stools?' Alison asks as I'm tapping away at the computer.

I reel back, shocked that she would seek out my medical assessment in a matter this personal. Fortunately, it turns out she's still in pursuit of the catalogue lifestyle and is talking about breakfast bar accessories.

'How much are they?'

'Ninety pounds each. You can buy them out of the money you make from your book.'

'Alison, if you keep coming in here waving brochures under my nose when I'm trying to work there won't be a bloody book. If we go up on Sunday I will study stools until the cows come home. In fact on Monday I will enrol at the Stoke-on-Trent University of Interior Design and start a four-year degree in stool design.

'And on Tuesday I'll scour the shops and bring back a load of different stools for us to try out. Stool samples, I suppose you'd call them. Stool samples. D'you see what I did there? Stool samples. Oh, forget it.'

Wednesday. I talk to Andy about what we're going to do after the game if we get promoted. Strangely, he's insistent on celebrating with cava, not a drink readily associated with Stoke-on-Trent.

'Cava?' I ask.

'Cava,' he says. 'We should go into Stoke and soak up the atmosphere with a bottle of Cava, go back to Mum's for tea and then get down the Wolf.'

'Cava? Champagne's more upmarket if you want to go down that route.'

'No. I want cava.'

'Fair enough.'

Relaying this surreal conversation at work, the talk turns to people who say they don't have to drink to have a good time. Rich says these people are just too stupid to realise how miserable they are, and there's general agreement.

Thursday. The nagging tension is always there; a background hum that isn't just personal, it seems to have seeped through the bricks, concrete, glass and tarmac of the whole city. All of a sudden the thrum of the traffic has a muted note of caution, voices in the shopping centres are lower, and the rising number of replica shirts being worn feels like nothing more than bravado in the face of faltering confidence.

No-one seems to talk about Sunday's game in the hours of daylight, and we all go about our jobs and do the shopping and talk to each other pretty much as usual. But at night, usually after ten or eleven o'clock, when people who don't understand have gone to bed or are bustling around in the kitchen or watching TV, you might get a couple of brief texts.

'Bricking it for Sunday,' one says tonight.

'Absolutely cacking it,' says another.

You send one back saying something like: 'No problems' or 'In the bag. We are Stoke.'

No justification is needed or expected in these soothing replies; their function is simply to spread reassurance to people debilitated by having to cope with a strange, additional low-level but constant insecurity in their lives, like an unseen hand reaching out and squeezing your arm in the dark as the ship climbs the biggest wave yet.

Friday. Every day more of the stories that make these occasions great keep coming out. The press and the radio have caught the mood, and the national spotlight heaves northwards and focuses on our poor beleaguered and belittled club and city with an intensity that almost makes you squint.

People who have upped sticks from grey, impoverished Stoke-on-Trent and emigrated to Spain, Australia and America in search of a better standard of living, adventure, sunshine, love or themselves are finding it's not as easy as they thought to shrug off their roots. For some of them, it is the first time in decades they've felt the pull of the Potteries, but here they are, without tickets for the game, landing at Manchester or Heathrow or Stansted or driving or walking off the ferry at Dover and succumbing to the nagging, magnetic, inescapable pull of their birthplace.

You do everything you can to avoid tempting fate, and

today I have a mild panic attack about whether the club has already doomed us to failure by organising an open-top bus for the triumphant tour of the city on Monday or Tuesday. If they have, even if some office minion had done it on the qt, surely that would mean we will lose on Sunday and Hull will win.

Even a casual phone call expressing an interest could scupper everything. ('Hello, is that Syd's Celebratory Vehicles (Stoke-on-Trent) Ltd – open-top buses and motorised Santa sleighs a specialty? Suppose a friend of mine wanted to enquire, nothing more you understand, about the availability of an open-top bus?')

I sincerely hope anyone trying to feed the family and pay the mortgage by renting out open-top buses in the Potteries has long since diversified. No-one's going to retire to the Bahamas on a 1972 League Cup win and a Division Two play-off final victory in 2002.

Saturday. I'm sitting here watching Sky Sports News go round and round interminably, as if I expect some sort of revelation to scroll across the screen if I stare at it long enough, some coded message confirming success tomorrow is our destiny and our right. All I get is sore eyes, though, and heartburn from a whisky intake this week which has done little to calm Alison's fear that she is married to George Best's less well-behaved love-child.

We watch *Match Of The Day* and a camera shooting from knee level follows the Man United and West Ham players walking on to the Old Trafford pitch, with tier after tier after tier of faceless fans in the background. Next season it could be us filing out with Ronaldo, Giggs, Scholes, Rooney and the rest of them and the enormity of the prospect hits me afresh.

'I just can't imagine it,' says Alison. 'I've tried visualising it, but I just can't and that's why I don't think we'll do it.'

I can't imagine it either, and my nerves are shot to pieces, but I know we're a better team than Leicester and I know we have a team which, all season, when we absolutely posi-bloody-tively had to get something out of the game, have delivered the goods.

I'm lying in bed thinking about how Leicester's and Stoke's fortunes have been inextricably linked in the recent past. It's no great coincidence – no matter who we were playing on the last day we would search for clues and omens in previous encounters. It was Leicester we lost to in the play-offs in 1996, although we should have won comfortably on the balance of play.

They went on to have one of the most successful spells in their history, winning the League Cup twice, reaching the final on another occasion and playing the likes of Athletico Madrid in the UEFA Cup. Some Stoke fans see victory on Sunday as our destiny – to exact revenge on the team that robbed us of glory twelve years ago, to reclaim what is rightfully ours, while I'm more your glass is half empty sort of guy and I see the fact that we're playing Leicester as a bad sign, a darkening cloud on the week's horizon.

As I lie in bed I realise the occasional stabbing pain in my chest has developed into a constant ache. Bloody typical, I think through rising panic, you wait twenty-three years for this and you're going to miss it because you'll be dead of a heart attack or in the hospital with five surgeons peering into your bloody cavity and scratching their heads.

One impressive but slightly alarming bout of flatulence later and I feel much better.

CHAPTER 26

Sunday. Ash's wife, who is eight months pregnant, walks into the room, panic-stricken, with a dark wet patch spreading down her trousers.

'My waters have broken,' she says. 'We've got to get to the hospital *now*.' Ash calculates he can make it to the maternity ward, get hold of his mum and mother-in-law and still be at the Britannia in time for kick-off. As he's frantically looking for his car keys, Zoe collapses into laughter and tells him she poured a glass of water over herself as a joke.

'Your face,' she says. 'Your face.'

It's that sort of day. Everyone's got a story. Andy wants to get the train down so we can go for a drink, but engineering work means it would involve catching connecting buses. He's not prepared to take the risk that some sort of public transport screw-up will leave him stranded in Stafford, so he spends the best part of three hours cycling the thirty miles from Manchester.

It's been raining torrentially on and off all morning, and the symbolism is all wrong. In my mind I've played out this day a thousand times, and every time it has been sunny and warm, the rich spring light reflecting off the thousands of freshly-washed replica kits in the crowd. My confidence is waning.

Today will be the biggest crowd ever seen at the Britannia Stadium, and the backstreet entrepreneurs are out in force for the first time I can remember, hawking soggy promotion flags, scarves, T-shirts and badges.

Inside, it's just beautiful. I walk from the concourse of

the Boothen End, turn left onto the stairs and the stadium opens out, full to bursting, flags everywhere, and, except for one corner which is solid blue with Leicester fans, the whole place is a shifting mass of red and white. As I turn my back on the pitch to climb the steps towards my seat, the sun breaks through the clouds for a few seconds, briefly illuminating my friends and the faces around us which have become so familiar over the years. I stick my chest out and join in the singing as I'm still heading upwards to row twenty-two.

Here we are then. Two p.m., Sunday, 4 May. Twenty-three years distilled into one match. A single game to wipe the slate clean, a single game to reach out to the lost generation, a single game for redemption. The ref blows his whistle and we're off.

Even now, just the day after the game, I can't remember that much about it.

This is no meaningless, end-of-season game for Leicester, either – they are in a desperate struggle with Southampton, Coventry and Sheffield Wednesday to avoid being the team to fill the last relegation spot – so their fans are in full, urgent voice and, to begin with, the stadium walls seem to bulge and flex with the pressure of the combined sound. I know Leicester hardly touched the ball for the first twenty minutes or so, and our players seem nerveless and determined, winning corner after corner and free kick after free kick.

But we never really look like scoring, and the rapidly growing knots in the pits of twenty-five thousand stomachs start to choke off songs before they catch and spread. Everywhere you look there are supporters listening to radios with one earpiece in and the other dangling uselessly. Every so often you see one of them clamp his finger to his empty ear in an attempt to hear where the next report is coming from, scowling at the noise around them. Or one will shoot out a hand and punch his neighbour's leg.

'They're going to Portman Road,' he says, and he looks round to make sure everyone has grasped the import of the news.

'What's he say?'

'They're going to Portman Road.'

'There's been a goal at Portman Road?'

'No. I don't know. They're going there next.'

'Who's scored? Has someone scored? What's the score?'

'I'm not sure, we're just waiting for ... are they there yet? What's happening? Who's scored?'

'No-one's scored, still nil-nil,' says the bloke with the radio. 'It was just an update.'

I presume, possibly wrongly, that technological advances are not just meant to make rich people richer, but they are surely also meant to enhance and simplify all our lives. Okay, those predictions in the 1960s and 1970s that we would all only need to work two days a week by 1990, leaving the other five free for us to play with our gravity cars or personal jet packs or to sit in our massage chairs swishing the remote control curtains back and forth, were obviously just a tad wide of the mark, what with us all working more hours than ever for the privilege of not being able to afford a gallon of petrol.

But surely we could reasonably expect, with satellites chattering away to each other in outer space, with wireless mobile technology, with the sum total of all human knowledge available in milliseconds at the press of a return key, surely we should be able to find out the footy scores in a timely fashion.

Can we buggery. Some people are listening to local stations on their mobile phones, some are listening to national stations on their digital radios, some are tapping into the internet and others are relying on friends and family for a steady beep beep of text messages. Gone are the days when there was about one bloke per stand who, with a radio held to his ear for the entire game, was the fount of all knowledge when we needed to know what was happening in other matches. At the Victoria Ground, the guy with the wireless in our block was known as Tranny Man, I presume referring to his precious transistor radio rather than any enthusiasm for cross-dressing, but I could be wrong.

Today, the result of this proliferation of communication technology is almost total confusion. News comes at you from all sides, but it's impossible to keep track. Someone might tell you Crystal Palace have scored, and then five minutes later someone else will tell you the same thing. Does that mean it's 2-0, or is someone tuned to a station that has only just reported the first goal or looking at a website which is slow to update?

I'm having as much difficulty keeping up as I do making head or tail of one of Lewis's particularly complex cases, and I try to just concentrate on the game in front of me.

It's impossible, but at 2.25 p.m. the Leicester fans go bananas, and for once everyone's technology is in agreement: Sheffield United have taken the lead against Southampton. This is great news for us as well. Leicester now only need to draw to stay up, so rather than throwing everything at us and risk being caught on the break, surely they will play for the point and we will do the same in some sort of unspoken gentleman's agreement that will see us all go home happy. In fact, sod a gentleman's agreement, the lawyers should as we speak be drawing up a contract to be signed by both managers and all players over champagne and vol-au-vents at half-time.

Ten minutes later, though, Southampton equalise and we're back to square one. As it stands, Leicester would stay up on goal difference, but they can't run the risk of Southampton going ahead and damning them to away days at Hartlepool and Hereford next season.

As the half-time whistle blows, the tension is almost beyond tolerance, and in an attempt to keep my sanity I keep reminding myself that Hull have to win at Ipswich – the team with by far the best home record in the Championship – and we have to lose in order for the unthinkable to happen.

After the restart, Fuller's effort from about two yards is somehow kept out and Liam Lawrence has a claim for a penalty turned down. Then at 3.15, Southampton go ahead, so now Leicester know they are going down unless they beat us. Almost immediately the tide begins to turn, and Leicester start to dominate, desperate for the goal that will save them. They hit the post, and other goal-bound efforts are blocked by Stoke players flinging themselves in the firing line. Around this time a group of Stoke fans in the corner of the West Stand starts to celebrate. It catches and spreads. Only Ipswich scoring against Hull would get this joyous reaction, but no-one near me can confirm it. I scan the East Stand and another group of fifty or sixty is bouncing up and down in uncontainable delight. We're all half in and half out of our seats, peering left and right and up and down trying to find out what the hell's going on. Meanwhile the roar spreads then falters and then spreads again, but still people near me are shaking their heads, insistent Ipswich are still drawing with Hull. They're right, and eventually the noise subsides and people sit back down, massaging their foreheads in a vain attempt to dissipate the tension.

At 3.22 p.m., Sheffield United equalise, meaning Southampton would now go down in Leicester's place, but once again Leicester must still go all out for the win to be sure.

The match is perfectly teed up for us to blow it. Leicester need a goal and look like they could get it at any time, Hull are desperate to score too and we're looking decidedly shaky at the back. Until this point I had no idea a football game could cause completely paralysing fear, and I sit with my arms folded tightly, with absolutely no idea how I'm going to get through the next thirty minutes.

Alison refused to come to the game because she's only been to a couple all season and she doesn't want to be branded as the jinx, the albatross around the neck-end of our season, if we lose.

She's watching the game on Sky and sends me a text: 'Feel sick and Leicester fans are crying,' and it hits me once again how much this stupid, beautiful sport means to us all. This game must be terrible to watch for anyone without an allegiance – and there are plenty of neutrals to confirm this in the days ahead – but to true Stoke and Leicester fans it has an awful, inescapable drama that is as spellbinding as it is terrifying.

At about 3.30 p.m. on Sunday, 4 May, 190.7 miles away from the Britannia Stadium, Alan Lee heads into the corner from twelve yards and Ipswich are beating Hull 1-0.

The suffocating blanket of tension is lifted and the relief is intoxicating. We stand up, lift our heads, raise our hands towards the sky and sing like birds released. It would take a complete disaster now, a catastrophe of proportions unheard of even in Stoke City's recent history, to keep us out of the Premier League. In the next twenty-five minutes, Leicester would have to score against us and Hull would have to score twice against Ipswich, and we all know it's over. Carlo Nash has to make a couple of great saves, but we're too busy singing and smiling to care.

We know the game is over half a second before the shrill blast of the final whistle reaches the Boothen End because Richard Cresswell falls to his knees, arms raised and eyes closed, oblivious to the thousands upon thousands of Stoke fans sprinting from every direction onto the pitch. Liam Lawrence sprints full pelt towards one wave of supporters, and even at this distance it's obvious he's close to tears, and Carl Dickinson, the lad from down the road who supports Stoke and came through the academy here as a boy, looks as if his body, his flesh-and-bone physical being, is just completely inadequate to deal with the emotions he is feeling.

He sprints towards thousands of delirious Stokies at the same rate they are tear-arseing towards him. Just a few yards before impact, he plants his feet, raises his arms and opens his mouth to scream at the very moment he is engulfed and overrun. I see his elbow emerge here, a hand there and finally his big, grinning face before I completely lose him thirty seconds later.

I don't see or can't remember the other players' reactions or how Tony Pulis deals with this spectacular vindication of his vilified methods because my eyes are screwed shut, my fists are clenched and my arms point to the sky.

A minute later I look around at my friends and the familiar faces of the people who sit near us who aren't on the pitch; eyes bright with emotion, we all look a bit different somehow, softer and slightly confused, uncertain how to deal with simple victory after the complexities of the last two hours. We all shake hands and shake our heads knowingly at each other as we do, and it feels a bit like New Year's Day. I'm walking down the steps towards the pitch with Andy and Ash when, without warning, it's all I can do to stop myself from crying.

We've left cousin Dave in his seat for a minute, getting to grips with his emotions. His dad, a Stoke fan, died a couple of months ago, and the mixed feelings must be all but impossible to reconcile. Over the next few days, hundreds of stories like this will emerge; a long, sad list of loved ones who never quite made it through the barren years. It's been a long season, and I realise how we've all been left a little fragile and vulnerable after coping with the despair, hope, boredom, uncertainty, anger and ultimately joy of the last nine months.

Leicester are relegated. For the first time in their 124-year history, they will be in the third tier of English football. Later, their manager, Ian Holloway, will say he has let down his family and everybody associated with the club. But now, the Leicester fans are applauding their stunned and broken players from the pitch. A minute later I realise they're still applauding, but now it's us they're clapping – our team and our fans – and again it's all I can do to stop the tears from falling.

CHAPTER 27

We don't quite know what to do now we're on the pitch.

Fifteen years ago we would be pushing through the heaving mass pressing up to the stand where we think the players might come out. Now, though, we potter about on the periphery and, in a horrifying reminder of the catastrophic effects of the ageing process, Andy merely makes appreciative comments about the quality of the grass and wonders aloud how they keep it in such good condition.

In my defence, I tell him to shut up before, quite rightly, we are hounded out of the stadium (although, if I'm honest, I do have a surreptitious toe of the turf when he's not looking and make a mental note to check if there are any groundkeeping tips on the Stoke website).

We mill around, taking a few pictures on our mobiles or the cameras that we've brought and then it feels natural to drift over to the Family Stand. Andy takes CJ, William and James back on to the pitch and I climb up to find my sister, my two brothers-in-law and my father-in-law. Ian – the same Ian who, at the end of last season, said, in all seriousness, he was sick of football, of all the money in the game, of the lack of loyalty shown by players and the poor example being set to his kids by diving, spitting, arguing players and swearing, spitting, arguing fans – cried for five minutes solidly after the final whistle.

Neil, a Stoke fan by marriage, just looks relieved it's all over, Karen looks five years younger and John has one of those distant, serene half-smiles you generally associate with Buddhist monks meditating the steps to nirvana on top of a Himalayan peak.

We stand there, high above the restless carpet of people and flags on the pitch, and enjoy the glorious anti-climax of it all, the lazy, limp, third-day-of-your-holiday feeling when you suddenly discover that you've got nothing left to worry about.

Eventually the players and Peter Coates appear high up in the West Stand and you can almost taste the desperate gratitude behind the cheering and the songs from the fans.

'One Peter Coates, there's only one Peter Coates,' we sing, and I can't help grinning as I wonder how many of us were in the Boothen End a few years ago chanting 'Coates out! Coates out!' jabbing our fingers towards the impassive figure in the posh seats and baying for blood on the boardroom carpet.

The chairman gives a short, low-key speech and lets the players take the adulation, while Tony Pulis fades into the background. In the brief interviews he gives after the game the manager is matter-of-fact and businesslike, but you can still tell how much it means to him, and he looks like a man relieved of a terrible burden. It's hardly surprising, I suppose.

He's been carrying the weight of unrealistic expectations for longer than most people could stand, wading against an undercurrent of hostility which must have been emotionally debilitating, no matter what he says to the contrary.

If I was Peter Coates or Tony Pulis, I would find it difficult not to use the local, national and international media frenzy around the Britannia Stadium to stick my middle finger up to all the moaners, doubters and know-it-alls like me who criticised almost every move they made and who were unwilling to give up our fears and ingrained prejudices even in the face of overwhelming evidence that things were going to be different this time.

Would I be big enough to let all the crap I had gone

through for this club slide past unchallenged? I don't know. Maybe. Maybe promotion to the Premier League and a cheque for £60m are a big enough 'screw you' without the need for words.

The truth is, though, you don't get the impression either Peter Coates or Tony Pulis hold a shred of resentment towards us or even the smallest desire to say 'We told you so,' and deep down the sheepish majority are relieved we have been allowed to share – and even take some of the credit for – this incredible achievement without having a guilt trip laid on us.

Three days before the Leicester match, a season ticket holder appeared in *The Sentinel* trying to sell off ten thousand red cards for charity. They were bought for the narrowly-averted anti-Pulis protest in October, 2006. And at the Colchester match a week ago, the travelling Stokies unfurled a large banner saying 'PULIS OUT'. The O had been turned into a smiley face. It's taken two years, but Peter Coates and Tony Pulis have well and truly found redemption – whether they were looking for it or not.

Half an hour later and I'm walking through town with Andy. The pubs are full to bursting, the pavements outside blocked by fluid groups of drinkers who've either been at the game and made it back before us or people who couldn't get tickets and have been watching in the boozer. Passing cars honk their horns in celebration, and each one is greeted with a cheer and raised flags, pint glasses, lager bottles or fists.

Local politicians, regeneration leaders, marketing experts and academics have all talked about what promotion to the Premier League will mean to Stoke-on-Trent: millions of pounds pumped into the local economy by the thousands of additional away fans we will get every week; millions more from targeted marketing campaigns persuading some of these to stay overnight and visit local attractions; thousands of jobs as national and international investors become aware of this small city just off the motorway halfway between Manchester and Birmingham; and a thriving artistic and cultural sector as we all flock to theatres, galleries and Michelin-starred restaurants to get rid of some of our newly-won disposable income.

With all the giddy excitement, I half expect to see the pavements already laid out with chrome café tables, casual but wealthy-looking customers sipping espressos or skinny frappacappamoccaccinos and checking their share portfolios in the *Financial Times* while they tell their friends about the Ibsen play they went to see last night with Jocasta.

Walking past O'Leary's, past the Wellington, past the Sutherland, past the Commercial, the pavements are still dominated by groups of men drinking pints and in various states from mellow celebration to a couple of drinks away from falling into the road. Even as we lean into the steep hill heading up towards Penkhull, editors in Melbourne, Sydney, Tel Aviv, Vancouver, Durban, Kingston, Buenos Aires, New York City, Los Angeles, Paris and Stockholm are watching the news come through the wires and writing about a 0-0 draw in a different time zone between two teams their readers may barely have heard of.

And tomorrow nearly every national UK paper will have pictures from the game on the front and back pages: panoramic shots of the Britannia Stadium, the pitch just an expanse of red and white; a Leicester fan in tears; an ecstatic father and son, both with their faces painted, Richard Cresswell on his knees; Carl Dickinson, surrounded by fans, his unbridled roar of delight frozen forever.

Does it really matter that in the morning millions of people will be reading about us with detached interest in the departure lounge at Heathrow? In cafés on Deansgate in Manchester, at the Albert Dock in Liverpool, by the side of the river in Nottingham or in pubs in Camden Town?

Does it make any difference to the way they think about Stoke-on-Trent and are they now planning fortnight breaks with the family to see the cosmopolitan delights of North Staffordshire and making mental notes to talk to the boss on Monday about relocating the business to Fegg Hayes?

Probably not, but it makes *us* feel differently about our city and ourselves, and maybe that's the really important thing.

We walk on past the Terrace and into the quiet of the bar at the Marquis, which used to be our local before we moved after Harry was born.

Alison and I would meet there every Friday after work, chat about the week and get quietly tipsy as the mix of customers changed from the let's-have-a-quick-pint-at-five brigade to the Friday-night-on-the-town crowd. Alison had much further to come than me, so I was usually there first and I'd sit there reading my *Sentinel*. When she arrived I'd say I'd only had a pint of Carling when really I'd had two pints of Stella. We'd leave our cars in the car park and walk the few hundred yards downhill to home. It was a great way of shutting the door on the working week and I miss it.

I also miss those clear mornings when I was on an early shift and the sun was just rising. Turning left at the Marquis roundabout, and coming over the brow of Honeywall, you could see just about the whole of the city sleeping in the valley stretching out below you. Only the tallest or closest or highest buildings would be silhouetted against the beautiful sweeps of grey, red, pink and lilac, and sometimes the air was so still the discharge from the incinerator chimney would rise dead-straight through the horizontal bands of colour and you would have to really crane your neck to see where it merged with the lightening sky.

I don't miss having my fence set on fire on a weekly basis by kids from the school a hundred yards away from our house, mind you, but still, it's nice to be back.

Thankfully, Andy's forgotten his brief obsession with sparkling white wine and we have a couple of sparkling yellow lagers in the calm frosted-window light of the bar, a gentle clink of our glasses bringing the curtain down on yet another season.

'Cheers.'

'Well done, mate.'

'Yeah, good work,' we say, in mutual appreciation, as if we have been on the pitch, sliding in with last-ditch tackles and defending the posts on corners.

A few Mondays ago I was at the stadium queuing for tickets for the Colchester beamback. The line was three hundred yards long and, judging by the way most of us turn our back on the TV cameraman there to record the build-up to the big game, very few of us had been completely frank with the boss about our whereabouts.

I noticed Leon Cort trotting head down into the ground, and he looked so young, like a boy, really, although I think he's in his late twenties. As he glanced shyly up the long line of people, did he momentarily think, as I did, how incredibly foolish it was that for nearly all these people, how he plays in a few days – this boy with no real emotional connection to this blustery collection of towns – will help shape one of the most important days in their lives? Some of them are nearly three times his age, some will have fought in wars and seen the friend standing next to them disappear in a fizz of blood and tissue, some will have been to prison, been divorced, had children and grandchildren, sat helpless in plastic chairs next to hospice beds as their wives passed away, survived terrible accidents, been promoted and sacked and loved and hated. But just then – just at that precise moment – none of these things were at the forefront of our minds. At precisely that moment we were all looking down the line and silently urging this stranger to help change our lives for the better and contribute to memories that will stay with us forever.

I suppose I was asking myself whether players at this level, on five or ten or twenty thousand pounds a week, really give a crap whether they win or lose, as long as they do well enough to keep hold of their ticket on the gravy train and maybe catch the eye of a club who can afford to pay even more for their loyalty.

Even before the Colchester game, though, I know the answer – at least for this bunch of players. For a sizeable proportion of this season they haven't played well, but they've never looked like they don't care, and the instinctive reactions in the hour after the final whistle on Sunday just confirm it – it matters.

Maybe more to them than to us, in fact. It's easy to be melodramatic about the importance of this season to our lives (twenty-three years of hurt ... a lost generation ... coming in from the wilderness ... destiny ... fate ... the sleeping giant awakes) but I'd already renewed my season ticket before I knew if we were going up or even going to make the play-offs, and so had more-or-less every other season ticket holder, just as we had all done a year ago when it was pretty obvious everything was going to pot.

Over the past twenty-three years, have I felt like following cricket or rugby instead, or contemplated going to salsa classes on a Saturday afternoon or taking a computer course or, God forbid, learning to ride a horse, or even just staying at home and watching the scores come in on the telly? Not once, as far as I remember.

Can I honestly look back and say I haven't got a stadium-full of priceless memories from two decades of wandering aimlessly in the footballing wilderness? The last game at the Victoria Ground, turning the light out on the ground which had been our home for a hundred and nineteen years, a record in English football.

Weekends in London to see us playing Reading in the league or Arsenal in the cup, a weekend on the Isle of Man watching a pre-season tournament. Gillingham away, Bournemouth away, Forest away, Crewe away, beating Man United, major followings to see minor trophy victories at Wembley, the play-off win at the Millennium Stadium, avoiding relegation on the last day of the season. Even humiliating defeats make for great stories when the shame has passed.

But, from a distance, these triumphs and disasters aren't really that important to me either. It's the whole familiar process of going to the match, year in, year out, the decades of little peaks and troughs which provide the framework for everything else going on in my life, a rare constant in a generally disorganised and hotch-potch existence. And it's the faint jolt of excitement you get even in the most miserable of seasons when you remember Saturday is a home game and you've got more to look forward to than going to the supermarket or Ikea. Am I saying that the main reason I love watching Stoke is because it's better than shopping? No, although, let's be honest, that's a pretty good reason in itself. It's because of the people, the ritual, the habit, the beers with friends, the feeling of belonging, the civic pride, the banter and the passion I have for the sport as a whole.

For all of these reasons and a hundred more, there is never any doubt about me renewing my season ticket, no matter how rubbish we are. It's as if my dad awakened some sort of genetic defect when he gave me that Everton kit all those years ago, and you'd have the same result persuading me to stop breathing as asking me not to go to the game – the process is as natural and as necessary.

If you ever need cheering up, you could do worse than sitting in the car park of Morrisons in Stoke-on-Trent.

It's twenty-four degrees, there isn't a cloud in the sky, and the hillock to my left that was once a waste heap is capped with a thick layer of dazzling daisies and buttercups. The warm breeze smells of clutch and brake fluid and it ruffles and snaps the three Stoke banners I can see sticking out of car windows.

The trees dotted around the car park are in blossom and the dark green firs look positively Mediterranean against the light blue of the sky.

I'm scanning the paper and enjoying the gentle heat of the sun coming through the open window.

Every so often, *The Sentinel* runs old back pages from the seventies or eighties. The hairstyles are longer or shorter, moustaches are omnipresent or absent, shorts are shiny or matt, tight or baggy, but the words and the highlights are the same – the free kicks, the controversial penalty, the scrambled goal, the weather: the ebb and flow of a game long gone. Every match unique yet almost identical to hundreds that have gone before or that have yet to be played. It dawns on me that the mud and the grunts and the tackles and the goals aren't the real story; neither is the real story to be found in the unending columns of newspaper reports across the world.

It isn't the players who stay at the club for a few weeks or months or years before packing the Louis Vuitton luggage and moving on up the road, and it isn't even the injury-time goal to win the Champions League, the 4-3 victory after being 3-0 down or the astonishing beauty of a crisp, clean finish at the end of an eight-man move.

The real story is the people reading the reports in supermarket car parks or on the tube, the fans who turn instinctively to the back pages, the dads, mums and kids who turn out to watch their teams in Liverpool, Merthyr, Worcester and Dundee, in Rouen, Bremen and Palma, in Nairobi, Lima, Nanchang, Hyderabad, Melbourne and Stoke.

We are the story, beginning, middle and end – the anonymous millions behind the greatest game in the world.

Other books from SportsBooks

Charlie Hurley: The Greatest Centre Half the World has Ever Seen
Mark Metcalf

Charlie Hurley was voted Sunderland's Player of the Century in 1979, ten years after ending a brilliant career. A Republic of Ireland International, Charlie arrived from Millwall in 1957 and began his Sunderland career on the wrong end of a 7-0 demolition, including an own goal from Hurley himself. He stayed for 12 years and played 402 games. The title, Hurley is quick to stress, comes from a song the Roker Park faithful used to sing about him.

9781899807 69 7
Price £17.99
Hardback

Modern Football is Rubbish
Nick Davidson & Shaun Hunt

The authors are going through a midlife crisis as far as football is concerned. Now they've reached early middle-age they are wondering what has happened to the beautiful game. Where have all the muddy pitches gone they wonder. They wallow in nostalgia for 3 pm Saturday kick-offs and cup upsets and they rant against inflated egos, spiralling salaries and satellite TV. And they wonder about men in tights and gloves.

9781899807 71 0
Price £7.99
Paperback

The World at their Feet: Northern Ireland in Sweden
Ronnie Hanna

The story of Ireland's first trip to the World Cup when, despite being the smallest country, they reached the quarter-finals. Ronnie Hanna also wrote *Six Glorious Years: Following Northern Ireland 1980–86*

9781899807 74 1
Price £7.99
Paperback

Memories of George Best

Chris Hilton & Ian Cole

Malcolm Brodie, of the *Belfast Telegraph* who covered George Best throughout his brilliant and ill-starred career, called this "the best Best book ever". The authors talked to many of the Manchester United star's contemporaries to find out the true story of the wayward genius.

9781899807 57 4
Price £14.99
Paperback

From Sheffield with Love

Brendan Murphy

Published on the 150th anniversary of Sheffield FC, the world's oldest football club. The book charts the rise of organised football in Sheffield and Nottingham, the two oldest centres of the game

9781899807 56 7
Price £8.99
Paperback

The Irish Uprising

Andy Dawson

The story of Roy Keane's first season at Sunderland, which ended with promotion to the Premier League.

9781899807 60 4
Price £10.99
Paperback

Wembley

Glen Isherwood

Everything you need to know about the 'old' Wembley. Every match ever played at the world's most iconic football venue is detailed here as well as appearances, scorers etc.

1899807 42 X
Price £14.99
Paperback

Accrington Stanley: the club that wouldn't die

Phil Whalley

Fan and writer Phil Whalley charts the comeback of Accrington Stanley the club which resigned from the Football League in the early '60s. After going bust they re-formed in 1968 and began an astonishing climb back to the League.

1899807 47 0
Price £16.99
Hardback

Europe United: a history of the European Cup/Champions League
Andrew Godsell
The story of the European Cup on its 50th birthday.

1899807 30 6
Price £17.99
Hardback

Growing up with Subbuteo: my Dad invented the world's greatest football game
Mark Adolph
The author writes about the colourful life of the man who invented Subbuteo and turned it into a world-wide success.

1899807 40 3
Price £7.99
Paperback

Fitba Gallimaufry
Adam Scott
All you need to know about Scottish football and a lot you don't!

1899807 45 4
Price £9.99
Hardback

Ha'way/Howay the Lads
Alan Candlish
The rivalry between Newcastle and Sunderland is legendary. This book give a report of every game.

1899807 39 X
Price £14.99
Paperback

Ode to Jol: A Spurs fan's diary
Alasdair Gold
A very funny look at what turned out to be Martin Jol's last season at White Hart Lane.

1899807 43 8
Price £12.99
Paperback

Raich Carter: the biography
Frank Garrick
Raich Carter had his career ruined by the Second World War but he was the only player to win FA Cup medals before and after it. He also led Sunderland to their last League title winning season in 1935–36.

1899807 18 7
Price £16.99
Hardback

The Complete Centre-Forward: Tommy Lawton, the authorised biography
David McVay & Andy Smith
Tommy Lawton was one of England football's greatest strikers despite, like Carter, losing six years to the war. He went on to manage Notts County and his colourful career and life shine through.

1899807 09 8
Price £14.99
Hardback

The 1908 Olympics: the first London Games
Keith Baker
The first London games were held after Rome dropped out following the eruption of Mount Vesuvius in 1906 meant funds for building Olympic facilities were diverted to Naples to help rebuild the city. This book concentrates on the important controversies, especially those between Great Britain and the USA. Keith Baker is an historian and sports devotee.

9781899807 61 1
Price £7.99
Paperback

The 1948 Olympics: how London rescued the Games
Bob Phillips

London once again came to the rescue of the Olympics. War-torn London, pock marked with bomb damage, provided the backdrop to the return of the Olympics. The competitors were housed in barracks, the British athletes used public transport to get to the venues and it poured down. Bob Phillips was for many years a member of the BBC radio athletics team and he has a deep knowledge of the Olympics.

9781899807 53 3
Price £16.99
Hardback

The Lion and the Eagle
Iain Manson

The story of the illegal bare-knuckle prize fight between Tom Sayers and John Heenan that gripped England and the USA in 1860. The fighters, their handlers and the spectators avoided the police to watch the contest which was held in the Hampshire countryside.
Iain Manson captures the robust flavour of the Victorian era with New York being brought to a virtual standstill as people clamoured for news about the fight.

9781899807 67 3
Price £17.99
Hardback

Newmarket: A year at the home of horseracing
Foreword by Frankie Dettori
John Carter

Author John Carter interviewed and shadowed fourteen racing personalities throughout a year at Newmarket, the home and headquarters of British horseracing, in a book supported by the racecourse. One of the subjects, star photographer Trevor Jones, also supplied the photographs which are featured throughout the book.

9781899807 62 8
Price £19.99
Hardback

Talking of Sport: The story of radio commentary
Dick Booth

It is hard to believe that radio commentary started only in 1921 when the world heavyweight title fight between Jack Dempsey and Georges Carpentier at New Jersey was relayed to the outside world. And even now, with sports TV channels springing up all the time, radio sports commentary goes from strength to strength.

Dick Booth is also author of a biography of the English long-distance runner Gordon Pirie, *The Impossible Hero*.

9781899807 64 2
Price £17.99
Hardback

Shergar and other friends: An anthology of horseracing poetry
Jim Anderson

The author was a contemporary of Lester Piggott as an apprentice jockey but an injury ruined his chance of a successful career. Instead he turned to journalism becoming a sports editor and feature writer on provincial and Sunday national papers, including some years writing football for the Sunday Express and Sunday People. He has now put his love of and knowledge about the turf into poetry and can claim that he rode Shergar's grandfather, Honeyway.

9781899807 63 5
Price £7.99
Paperback